ns
Heal A.

55 Raw, Plant-Based, Whole-Food Recipes
to Heal Your Body and Ignite Your Spirit

DANIELLE ARSENAULT

◆ FriesenPress

Suite 300 - 990 Fort St
Victoria, BC, V8V 3K2
Canada

www.friesenpress.com

Copyright © 2017 by Danielle Arsenault
First Edition — 2017

The author is not a medical practitioner and in particular does not present itself as being able to diagnose, treat, operate, or prescribe for any human disease, pain, injury, disability or physical condition and cannot and will not give medical advice. This book is not intended as a substitute for the medical advice of physicians. The reader should regularly consult a physician in matters relating to his/her health and particularly with respect to any symptoms that may require diagnosis or medical attention.

All rights reserved.

No part of this publication may be reproduced in any form, or by any means, electronic or mechanical, including photocopying, recording, or any information browsing, storage, or retrieval system, without permission in writing from FriesenPress.

ISBN
978-1-4602-9926-5 (Hardcover)
978-1-4602-9927-2 (Paperback)
978-1-4602-9928-9 (eBook)

1. COOKING, METHODS, RAW FOOD

Distributed to the trade by The Ingram Book Company

pachaVega
living foods education

Pachavega Living Foods Education ~ organic, plant-based education to heal your body and ignite your spirit!

We aim to inspire by living life from the heart and connecting to nature through the integration of a healthy lifestyle. At the core of this philosophy is nutritionally dense and deliciously flavourful, whole, plant-based food that is organically grown as close to home as possible.

www.pachavega.com

all photographs unless otherwise stated | Johanna Guinard and Danielle Arsenault

painting credits | © Alicia Severson
www.aliciaseverson.com
cover image and back image of beetroot
beetroot ~ page 13
seaweed ~ page 47
apples ~ page 72
chocolate ~ page 76

photo credits
Jessica Perlaza ~ pages 11/12, 14/15, 30/31
Stefano Tricanico ~ pages 4/5, 92/93, 96 (kayaking)
Jonathan Huyer ~ 82/83
www.huyerperspectives.com
Alain Denis ~ page 95
Seon Hwa Shim ~ page 97 (in the yellow rain pants)
Gillian Shepherd ~ pages 15/16, 17, 19
Jill LaBelle Sophie Shouldice ~ page 51
Shutterstock Photos ~ pages 17, 21, 27, 39, 46, 56, 57, 75, 78, 84, 86, 87

Health and healing foods weren't always my top priority but after being diagnosed with irritable bowel syndrome (IBS), along with gluten and dairy allergies back in 2005, I decided to delve head first into clearing up the major discomforts that my diet was causing. Armed with nothing but motivation to be a strong and healthy vegan in a non-vegan world, I have definitely required patience, imagination and education. With an eye for fresh foods, over the years I have discovered endless combinations and hidden secrets in nutrition, especially in raw, living foods.

In March of 2012, I completed a ukulele-infused album under my musical pseudonym, Mustache Fable. Later that year, I received a Permaculture Design Certificate as well as a Living Foods Lifestyle Education Certification at the Ann Wigmore Institute in Puerto Rico. My curiosity was piqued about the powers of a raw-food diet and lifestyle. In 2013 I furthered my studies and completed the 200-hour Raw Food Educator Program from Raw Foundation Culinary Arts Institute in Vancouver, Canada. My passion for healing had begun to bubble over and I knew it was my calling to strive to educate myself in depth about the healing power of whole foods and a cleansing lifestyle. In the fall of 2015 I became a Certified Colon Hydrotherapist. The next project is to go create an online school and develop Nutrition Night School, a weekly whole food preparation course held in the evenings.

For almost ten years, I travelled the world and discovered the isolated corners of more than twenty countries, as a rock climber, raw food chef and an English and Spanish teacher. I can become lost in the folds of nomadic travels now and then but I still find time to pursue my passions.

I have had the pleasure of collaborating with the lovely Jessica Perlaza and co-creating a vegan, gluten-free cookbook series inspired by seasonal whole foods. We call ourselves "the Kitchens of Pinch and Dash". Jessica is indeed an inspiration and I wouldn't be bringing this amazing collection of raw, vegan recipes to you without having known her. I am truly grateful for our shared vision and friendship.

Looking for some grounding roots, I founded Pachavega Living Foods Education in 2013 to inspire people to take charge of their happiness and health by eating mindfully. We offer whole foods, plant-based catering, nutritional consultation and chef certification including the most incredible 45-hour Healing Whole Foods Preparation Certificate and the 70-hour *Heal and Ignite* Raw Chef Certificate.

No matter how busy I get with projects, ukulele picking, playing in the garden, crossing mountain ranges, rock climbing, writing cookbooks, riding motorcycles, teaching and dreaming, I still have to eat. My boundless energy and creative drive are directly related to the food with which I nourish my body. After all, we are what we eat. I am chlorella, tahini, almonds and zucchini. Enjoy these recipes wholeheartedly and don't be afraid to tweak and experiment! This food is my creative expression, a gift to you.

in love & light, Danielle

Would you like Soup or Salad with that?   7

RED BEET BORSCHT	
WITH CASHEW SOUR CREAM	9
KAFFIR LIME CARROT SOUP	11
DR. ANN'S ENERGY SOUP	13
VIETNAMESE SHIITAKE SOUP	15
SPICY CHILI GARLIC PICKLE	15
"LOVE YOUR LIVER" SALAD	18
PAD THAI SALAD	19
TANGY GINGER KELP NOODLE SOUP	21
WASABI GINGER SUSHI SALAD	24
ITALIAN TOMATO SALAD	26

Save Room for Snacking   27

GRAWNOLA	30
RAWKIN' RAW PIZZA CRUST	31
CILANTRO PESTO	32
ZESTY TOMATO SAUCE	32
BASIL KALAMATA TAPENADE	33
PEAR LEMONGRASS SALSA	33
CURRIED GOJI BERRY RELISH	34
LENTIL DIPPERS	35
CURRY MANGO MUSTARD	36
PESTO PORTOBELLO MUSHROOMS	37
BLACK PEPPER TRUFFLE CASHEW CREAM	39
CAULIFLOWER MASH	41
TAHINI GRAVY	42
SWEET AND SMOKY COCONUT CHIPS	42
SAVOURY SAGE AND PECAN MEDLEY	43
SAVE THE SEA PÂTÉ	46
THE "PÂTÉ" FORMULA	46
KALE CURRY CRACKERS	47
THE "CRACKER" FORMULA	48
BASIC KRAUT	51
BOLD BRASSICA KRAUT	52
KOREAN KIMCHI	52

Delicious Desserts

53	
56	Luscious Lemon Cream Cake
57	Maca Carrot Cake with Vanilla Citrus Frosting
59	Chocolate Almond Pie
61	Pink Salted Caramel Coffee Cake
63	Real Fruit Roll-Ups
64	New Hazelnut Cream
66	Camu Camu Poppy Seed Nice Cream
68	Lavender Berry Surprise Pudding
69	Apple-Pear Walnut Crumble
72	Vanilla Dream Cream
72	Cinnamon Apricot Bread
73	Before-Dinner Mint Chocolates
75	Goji Berry Orange Fudge
77	No-Bake Coconut Cashew Cookies

To Quench Thirst

79	
81	Rooibos Kombucha Bubble Tea
84	Lemon Molasses Kefir
85	Fresh Brazil Nut Mylk
86	Chocolate Warrior Latte
87	Green Beauty Smoothie
88	Blood Builders Brew
88	Lust for Life Elixir

healing tips, tricks and unique superfoods to ponder a little longer

ORGANIC DOES MAKE A DIFFERENCE	5
THE DIRTY DOZEN AND CLEAN FIFTEEN	6
THE FIVE FLAVOURS ~ HOW TO FIX ANY RECIPE	9
THE STORY OF ANN WIGMORE AND THE MIRACLE OF WHEATGRASS	14
HEAL YOUR BODY AND IGNITE YOUR SPIRIT ~ SHARE, EXPERIMENT AND SPREAD THE LOVE	16
RAW FOODS LIFESTYLE AND GENTLE DETOXIFICATION	17
THE MEGA FLU FIGHTER MIX	21
LOVE, THE SECRET INGREDIENT	24
TOP FOOD COMBINING TIPS FOR BETTER DIGESTION	25
EAT A RAINBOW	29
SOAKING NUTS AND SEEDS? SAVE SOME TIME	30
TURMERIC ~ ANTI-INFLAMMATORY MAGIC	36
MEDICINAL MUSHROOMS AND IMMUNITY	37
NUT-FREE PLANT-BASED CUISINE	44
THE HEALTH BENEFITS OF SEAWEED ~ THE GREAT GRANDMOTHER OF ALL SUPERFOODS!	45
SOAKING AND SPROUTING	49
FERMENTED FOOD: GOOD FOR GUT HEALTH	50
MACA ~ THE MAGIC ADAPTOGENIC SUPERFOOD OF THE ANDES	58
WHAT IS CAMU CAMU?	66
ANTI-ANGIOGENICS ~ EAT TO COMBAT CANCER	68
HONEY; NECTAR OF THE GODS AND GODDESSES, LIQUID SWEETENER OF CHOICE?	70
WHO DOESN'T LOVE CHOCOLATE?	73
THE MIGHTY GOJI BERRY	75
ESSENTIAL OIL IN THE RAW PLANT-BASED DIET	76
COCONUT POWER!	77
KEFIR, A STORY OF INTRIGUE	83
SHILAJIT, ROCK WARRIOR	85
ACID OR ALKALINE; A DELICATE BALANCE	87
WHERE DO YOU GET YOUR PROTEIN?	91
ALL NATURAL BUG SPRAY	94

Why Raw?

The idea behind the power of raw food is that heating food over 118 degrees F destroys much of the food's nutrients, especially its vitamins, enzymes and life force. Raw food contains the natural enzymes to completely consume its food self. We need these enzymes to boost digestion and fight chronic disease. Your body can also create enzymes, but can only do so much. As we age, we begin to use up our store of enzymes and we cannot get this back. Along with the accumulation of toxins and our body's inability to create more enzymes as we age, we begin to see why chronic disease sets in. Cooking food also diminishes the natural life energy. A cooked seed won't grow, but a raw seed will. Another benefit is that the massive amount of energy that is takes to digest cooked food is freed up when you consume a raw foods diet. Some say raw foods are harder to digest, but ask yourself this, do you chew well enough? Incomplete chewing allows for indigestion because your body will see the big piece of food as a foreign object. When a food is chewed well enough, your body can break it down into its most usable components, not to mention that chewing allows the food to mix with your saliva which contains amylase, an enzyme that begins to breakdown carbohydrates. So, chew your liquids and liquefy your solids.

Some other benefits of eating a raw foods diet:

Regular bowel movements, thus allowing your body to process toxins more efficiently
Quicker thinking and increased energy and stamina
Stronger immune system
Less packaging
It contributes to a sustainable planet
A peaceful diet with respect for all living things

How long will it take?

Some people have the preconceived notion that raw food prep takes much more time than conventional cooking, but the opposite is true. Think of it as a reallocation of time. You might spend more time on a given day prepping food, but for the rest of the week, then you'll have freshness ready to grab and assemble in minutes. All you need is a little foresight and you can prepare several recipes one day a week. Most recipes in this book keep fresh for four to six days in the fridge so shred some carrots and beets, rinse some sprouts and soak some nuts and seeds. You'll have a veritable smorgasbord of sauces and dips as well as dehydrated goodies and fermented magic in your fridge anytime your tummy says "Feed me". All recipes will feed between two to six people with leftovers a delight. You may also freeze if you'd like to prolong the deliciousness.

Get excited to experiment in your kitchen and try new combinations with these ingredients. Taste as you go and share with those you love. Let your heart be open to the magic these new foods will bring to your life.

Enjoy this collection of recipes and be inspired to heal your body and ignite your spirit with the perfect nature of plant-based, whole-foods!

You can also find these two pages in AWAKE, the spring cookbook from the Kitchens of Pinch and Dash, but I felt it was important to mention it again here.

Volumes have been written about the ever-growing demand for organic food. These days we are over-informed, under-informed and misinformed about the inner workings of the food industry. A hot topic at dinner tables and farmers markets alike, the conversation about organics is one worth having.

organic does make a difference

Organic agriculture is a system of growing crops that increases, enhances and fosters the life of the soil. Conventional agriculture, on the other hand, depletes the soil and the life it sustains. Organic foods are grown without the use of fertilizers, herbicides or pesticides. One thing is certain: from soil to seed to sprout to plant, organic food is grown from the ground the way nature intended.

A common argument against buying organic is that it costs more than conventional food. Is it worth the extra expense? The truth is, every time you buy organic, you are investing in your health and in the health of the Earth. Believe it or not, conventional agriculture uses between thirty and sixty different kinds of pesticides to prevent fungi from growing and insects from dining on our favorite fruits and veggies. These chemicals are absorbed into the very core of the food itself and stick with it as it grows. When you ingest these foods, the chemicals lurking within become a part of you too.

These fruits and veggies listed on the next page are those considered to have the highest concentration of pesticide and herbicide residues. This list, according to the Environmental Working Group's shopper's guide to pesticides in produce, is updated online every year. If your budget is tight, plan on splurging on organic foods found in the "dirty dozen" list. Your body and the Earth will thank you. The list of "clean fifteen" fruits and vegetables ranks those that score the lowest in pesticide residue so you don't necessarily need to buy them organic. This makes sense since most have a thick skin that is removed before eating.

the dirty dozen

APPLES
CELERY
SWEET BELL PEPPERS
HOT PEPPERS
CHERRY TOMATOES
PEACHES
STRAWBERRIES
NECTARINES
GRAPES
SPINACH
LETTUCE
CUCUMBERS
POTATOES
KALE AND COLLARD GREENS

check www.ewg.org for the updated list

cauliflower mash and tahini gravy ~ page 41

the clean fifteen

PAPAYA
ONIONS
SWEET CORN
PINEAPPLES
AVOCADO
CABBAGE
SWEET PEAS
ASPARAGUS
MANGOES
EGGPLANT
KIWI
CANTALOUPE
SWEET POTATOES
GRAPEFRUIT
MUSHROOMS

Would you like Soup or Salad with that?

kaffir lime carrot soup ~ page 11

THE FIVE FLAVOURS

In Ayurvedic medicine and Traditional Chinese Medicine making food taste delicious considers the five flavours, sweet, salty, sour, bitter and umami. Let's add two more, fat and spice. A combination of these is the secret to making amazing dishes, bursting with flavour. Without this balance, you are left feeling unsatisfied and will inevitably say "something is missing".

HOW TO FIX ANY RECIPE

Too spicy? Add some fat, sweet or sour
Too sweet? Add some sour, salty or bitter
Too sour? Add sweet, salty, fat, bitter
Too bland? Add umami, sweet, salt, sour or some spice
Too salty? Add sour, fat, sweet
Too bitter? Add sweet, salty, sour
Needs spark? Add sour or umami such as lemon juice or tamari

red beet borscht

SALAD INGREDIENTS:
2 LARGE RED BEETS, PEELED AND SHREDDED
¼ HEAD NAPA CABBAGE, CHIFFONADE THIN (OR SHREDDED)
1 FUJI/GALA APPLE, SHREDDED
2 CARROTS, SHREDDED
½ CUP SPROUTED WILD RICE
½ CUP SPROUTED LENTILS

BROTH INGREDIENTS:
½ CUP MISO PASTE
1 TBSP LEMON JUICE
1 TBSP GLUTEN-FREE (GF) TAMARI
1 TSP ALLSPICE POWDER
5 CUPS BOILING HOT WATER, DIVIDED

GARNISH WITH MINCED FRESH DILL, A DOLLOP OF CASHEW
SOUR CREAM, A SPOONFUL OF KIMCHI AND RADISH SPROUTS

Procedure:

Combine all salad ingredients in a large bowl and mix well with tongs. Mix broth ingredients in 2 cups boiling hot water until dissolved. Divvy out the salad mixture in individual bowls then pour the miso mixture over top of each equally. Fill the bowls with the rest of the hot water and garnish with a dollop of cashew sour cream, a spoonful of kimchi, green onion and fresh dill.

Alternatively, you may blend all ingredients in a high-speed blender for a unique creamy soup. In this case, add 2 cups of room-temperature water before blending then blend for 4 minutes until steamy. Once in individual bowls, add the rest of the hot water and stir by hand. Garnish the same as above.

cashew sour cream

INGREDIENTS:
1 CUP RAW CASHEWS, SOAKED OVERNIGHT, DRAINED AND RINSED
¼ CUP WATER
1 TBSP LEMON JUICE
2 TSP APPLE CIDER VINEGAR

Procedure:
Blend in a high-speed blender until creamy and smooth.
Keeps fresh for a week in the fridge.

kaffir lime carrot soup

INGREDIENTS:

2 CUPS CHOPPED CARROTS
1 CUP MANGO (FRESH OR FROZEN)
2 CUPS YOUNG COCONUT MEAT
3 TBSP MAPLE SYRUP
2 GARLIC CLOVES
3 TBSP EXTRA-VIRGIN OLIVE OIL
2 TBSP LEMON JUICE
1 INCH SIZED PIECE OF GINGER
1 TBSP MINCED ONION
1 TBSP GF TAMARI
½ INCH FRESH TURMERIC
A PINCH OF SALT TO TASTE

FRESH BASIL, GREEEN ONION, JALEPEÑO AND EXTRA GINGER TO GARNISH

Procedure:
Prepare the lemongrass and kaffir lime leaf, place in 3 cups of boiling water and steep for 15 minutes. This flavourful broth will be the base of the soup. Remove lemongrass and lime leaves and add the broth, along with the rest of the ingredients to the blender and blend until steamy and smooth, about 3 minutes. Pour into bowls and garnish with a generous amount of basil chiffonade, green onion and chopped jalepeño peppers and extra ginger. Serve immediately while warm.

PREPARE IN ADVANCE:
1/2 CUP OF FRESH LEMONGRASS, CHOPPED FINELY.
1/4 CUP KAFFIR LIME LEAVES, CHOPPED FINELY.
6 CUPS OF WATER TO STEEP THE ABOVE INGREDIENTS

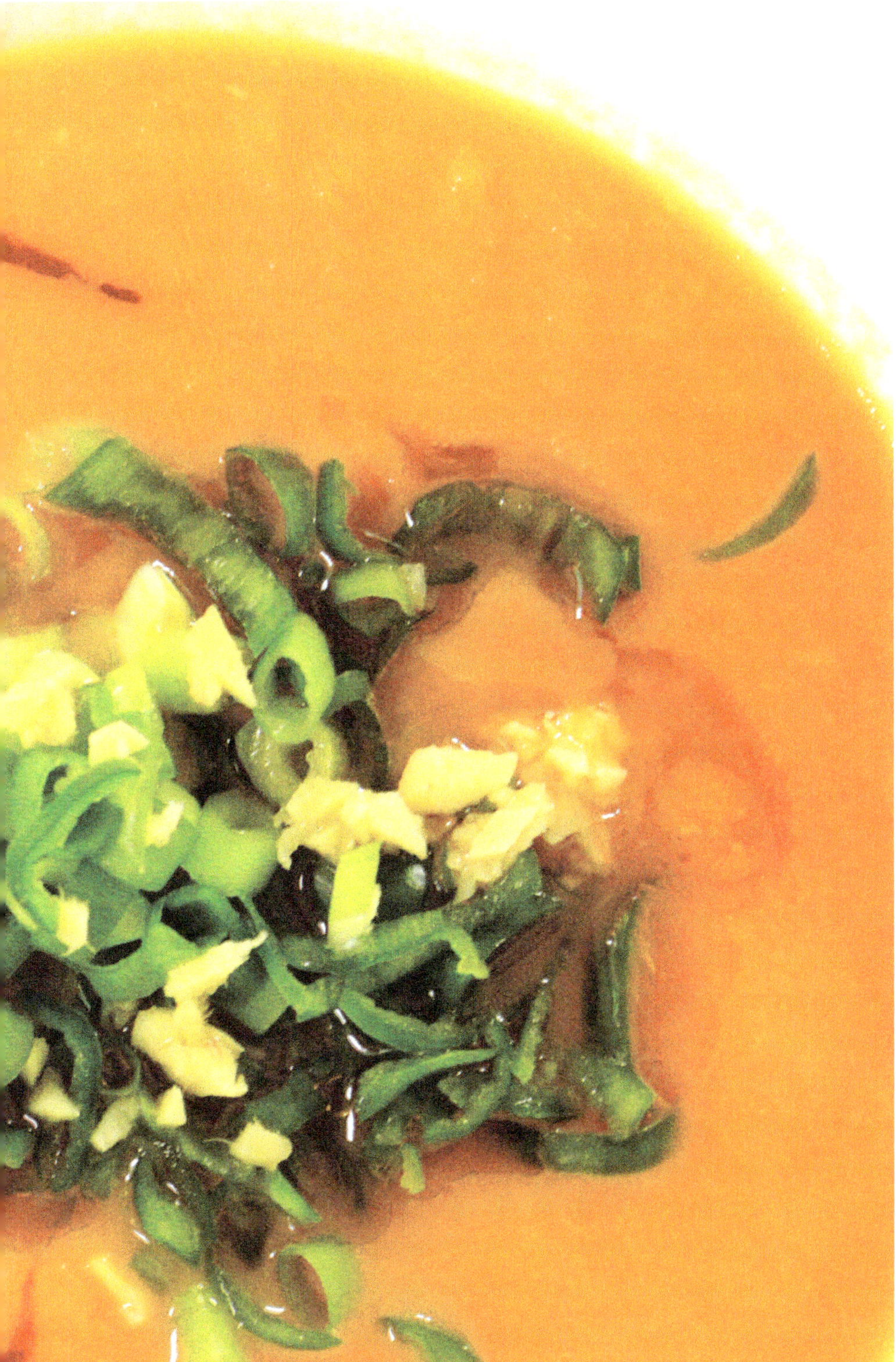

dr. ann's energy soup

Ingredients:
5 cups baby greens (kale, spinach, romaine)
1 cup green sprouts (broccoli or sunflower)
1 cup sprouted legumes (lentil, garbanzo)
2 avocados
1 apple for sweetness
4 tbsp seaweed, dulse or nori
2 ½ cup water
½ inch of ginger
1 lemon, juiced
sliced lemon for garnish

Procedure:
This soup becomes smooth and creamy in a high-speed blender. It can be eaten at room temperature (blend for one minute) or warm (blend for four minutes). Garnish with a slice of lemon.

"LET ME SHARE MY VISION WITH YOU: I SEE THE WORLD WITHOUT SICKNESS, SORROW OR MENTAL DISTURBANCES IN WHICH WE ARE LIVING IN PERFECT BALANCE AND ABUNDANT HEALTH AND HARMONY."

– DR. ANN WIGMORE

THE STORY OF ANN WIGMORE AND THE MIRACLE OF WHEATGRASS

Born in Lithuania in the early 1900's, Ann Wigmore grew up to influence hundreds of thousands of people's lives all over the world.

She felt abandoned by her parents when they left to immigrate to the United States, and she was left in the care of her grandmother, the village doctor. During the war, hard times forced the two of them to eat grasses and tree roots to survive. Eventually, at around the age of sixteen, she sailed abroad to reunite with her parents.

Throughout her life, Ann Wigmore suffered greatly. Having to endure gangrene and blood poisoning that put her into a coma would not be the worst of her battles with disease. She married at twenty-one but lived unhappily with sickness and eventually was diagnosed with a terrible case of colitis. Going from grasses and roots to the Standard American Diet did not help. She became more determined to heal herself naturally and reverted back to the teachings of her grandmother. She believed that eating sprouts and fresh, raw fruits, vegetables, seeds and nuts could have the power to heal the body of sickness. This eventually led her into excellent health, healing all trace of disease in her body. She was particularly fond of chewing on wheatgrass and noticed the profound benefits with its use. By purchasing a meat grinder at a local yard sale, she had her first wheatgrass juicer, strong enough to juice the fibrous fresh grasses she had been chewing on for so long.

She began to treat thousands of people with wheatgrass juice and finally founded the Hippocrates Health Institute as well as the Ann Wigmore Institute, both world renowned health institutes still to this day. Wheatgrass is widely regarded in the holistic health community at large to be a miracle elixir. It has been well documented over many years to improve the harmful effects of ailments such as anemia, arthritis, asthma, athlete's foot, bad breath, body odour, bleeding gums, burns, colitis, congested nasal passages, constipation, diabetes, diverticulitis, eczema, fatigue, gastritis, glaucoma, hemorrhoids, high blood pressure, inflamed mucous membranes, menstrual problems, obesity, pancreas and liver troubles, skin problems, sore throat, stomach ulcers, tooth pain, etc. Wow!

Because of her whole-hearted dedication to the health and wellness of all, her legacy lives on and she is still considered one of the biggest influences in natural healing that the world has ever known.

vietnamese shiitake noodle soup

spicy chili garlic pickle

INGREDIENTS:
5 CLOVES GARLIC
3 RED CHILIS
¼ CUP APPLE CIDER VINEGAR
2 TBSP OLIVE OIL

Procedure for the pickle:
Thinly slice chilis and garlic then in a mason jar, add the rest of the ingredients. Marinate for at least two hours before consuming. This spicy, quick pickle can be stored in the fridge for a week.

INGREDIENTS:
1 CUP FRESH SHIITAKE MUSHROOMS, SLICED
1 CUP MUNG BEAN SPROUTS
1 CUP KELP NOODLES, RINSED AND CUT WITH KITCHEN SHEARS
½ CUP SNOW PEAS, ENDS REMOVED AND SLICED DIAGONALLY
1 TBSP WHITE ONION, SLICED THIN
2 TBSP MISO PASTE
1 TBSP LIME JUICE
2 TSP CHOPPED CHIVES
2 TBSP MINT, CHIFFONADE
2 TBSP THAI BASIL LEAVES, CHIFFONADE

INFUSED BROTH:
6 WHOLE CLOVES, 1 CINNAMON STICK, 4 CARDAMOM PODS, 2 TSP CORIANDER SEEDS STEEPED IN 3 CUPS BOILING HOT WATER FOR 20 MINUTES.

Procedure:
Chop and prepare the shiitake, snow peas, onion, chives, mung bean sprouts and kelp noodles and place equal amounts in individual bowls. In a large glass bowl, infuse the broth by steeping the spices for twenty minutes. Once steeped, strain and remove spices from broth then mix in miso paste and lime juice and stir. Once the miso paste is dissolved, pour over the veggies in equal amounts, garnish with fresh mint and basil and let your core be warmed!

HEAL YOUR BODY AND IGNITE YOUR SPIRIT - SHARE, EXPERIMENT AND SPREAD THE LOVE

In a recent *Heal and Ignite* Raw Food Chef Certification course, a student created this amazing dish for her final Global Cuisine Menu Project which focused on Vietnamese cuisine. She used her previous knowledge of the traditional Vietnamese phở and made this absolutely mouth-watering soup! It was so good, I adapted it and then just had to include it in this book. It's great for chilly nights!

For more on the *Heal and Ignite* Raw Food Chef Course, visit www.pachavega.com/workshops/raw-chef-certification

RAW FOODS LIFESTYLE AND GENTLE DETOXIFICATION

With any gentle detoxification process, you'll need to eliminate certain things from your diet and lifestyle including milk and dairy products, gluten, caffeine, alcohol, refined sugars, bad fats (hydrogenated and partially-hydrogenated oils, heated and refined oils) and smoking. Once these are removed, the body has a fighting chance at clearing out toxins from the system.

Here are some tips and tricks to support the detoxification process:
~ Eat the following foods because of their astringent qualities. They will support the liver during detoxification - berries, lemons, black grapes, melons, bitter greens (arugula, dandelion)
~ Rebound: get on a trampoline and get that lymph moving!
~ Stay hydrated
~ Chew your food!
~ Avoid ice drinks as they suppress stomach secretions, thus affecting your ability to digest properly
~ Try colon hydrotherapy
~ Include a daily pro-biotic (capsules, sauerkraut). The role of gut flora is to influence your digestion. A healthy gut contains helpful or "friendly" bacteria that keeps harmful microbes in check. It is estimated that 90% of our immune system depends on this healthily balanced gut flora.

"love your liver" salad

Ingredients:
2 cups baby spinach / mixed baby greens
2 cups baby arugula
1 cup red radishes, sliced thin using a mandolin
¼ cup finely diced celery
1 avocado, chopped into small pieces
½ cup sprouted lentils
¼ cup pumpkin seeds (previously sprouted and dehydrated)
½ cup sprouted wild rice

Add wild edibles – depending on the season (rose petals, dandelion greens and flowers, juniper berries, clover, fiddleheads, or nettles)

A simple salad dressing:
1 garlic clove
1 tbsp dijon mustard
¼ cup apple cider vinegar
1 tbsp fresh lemon juice
1 tbsp liquid sweetener
½ cup hemp oil
Pink salt and pepper, to taste

Procedure:
Wild rice and lentils should be pre-sprouted. For instructions on how to do this, go to page 52.

Prepare salad ingredients by chopping, shredding, dicing, etc. Place all in a large mixing bowl.

Add sauce ingredients to a high-speed blender and blend on high until well mixed and creamy. Pour over salad and mix well using tongs.

pad thai salad

THE SAUCE:
3 TBSP LIME JUICE
3 TBSP WATER
2 GARLIC CLOVE
3 TBSP OF GF TAMARI
¾ CUP OF ALMOND BUTTER
3 TSP LIQUID SWEETENER
1 TBSP TOASTED SESAME OIL
2 TSP FRESHLY GRATED GINGER

THE SALAD:
KELP NOODLES, RINSED AND CUT
HANDFUL OF KALE, CHIFFONADE
¼ RED CABBAGE, CHIFFONADE THIN
1 ZUCCHINI, SPIRALIZED AND CUT
1 CARROT, PEELED OR JULIENNED
HANDFUL OF PUMPKIN SEEDS
FEW PINCHES OF CHOPPED GREEN ONION
BLACK SESAME SEEDS AND SPROUTS FOR GARNISH

Procedure:
Prepare salad ingredients by chopping, chiffonading, spiralizing, etc. Place all in a large mixing bowl except for sprouts and sesame seeds.

Add sauce ingredients to a high-speed blender and blend on high until well mixed and creamy. Pour over salad and mix well using tongs. Garnish with a sprinkle of black sesame seeds and sprouts. You may want to save some sauce for later. It will keep fresh in the fridge for 5 days.

20

tangy ginger kelp noodle soup

INGREDIENTS:
4 CUPS BOILING WATER
4 TBSP MISO PASTE
HALF A FRESH SERRANO CHILI, MINCED WITH SEEDS REMOVED
1 CLOVE GARLIC, MINCED
HALF THUMB OF FRESH GINGER, MINCED
1 TBSP GF TAMARI
1 PACKAGE KELP NOODLES, CUT WITH KITCHEN SHEARS
HANDFUL CILANTRO
HANDFUL CHOPPED SCALLIONS
HANDFUL SPROUTED LENTILS
JUICE FROM ONE LIME
DRIZZLE OF SPICY CHILI GARLIC PICKLE (RECIPE PAGE 18)

Procedure:
Combine broth ingredients with one cup of water in a high speed blender. In a separate bowl, cut the kelp noodles into smaller noodles with kitchen shears and then pour the broth over top. Divide the noodles and broth when softened into separate bowls for each person. Top off the bowls with hot water and garnish with freshly chopped cilantro and scallions and a drizzle of spicy chili garlic pickle.

THE MEGA FLU-FIGHTER MIX

Garlic, ginger, serrano chili, lime and cilantro all have detoxification properties and can help kick that cold before it even arrives.

~ Garlic has been revered all over the world and in many schools of nutrition due to its anti-bacterial, anti-fungal and anti-viral properties. It has the power to reduce yeast overgrowth and stimulate the production of glutathione which helps eliminate toxic build-up and strengthen our immune system immensely.
~ Ginger has been used for centuries to stoke digestive fires, calm indigestion, promote circulation and even facilitate the assimilation of nutrients.
~ Serrano chilies contain capsaicin, a chemical compound found in all spicy chilies, known to provide relief for IBS sufferers (it worked for me!) Capsaicin is also a potent anti-inflammatory and when ingested or even applied topically in a cream, has been proven to reduce pain, headaches and sinus symptoms.
~ Lime gives this soup a nice kick, but also stimulates the digestive system, enhances alkalinity and increases secretion of digestive juices.
~ Cilantro is known to chelate heavy metals, thus ridding the body of these unwanted toxins. Being a strong anti-oxidant, it also helps to lower the risk of oxidative stress in cells that may become carcinogenic.

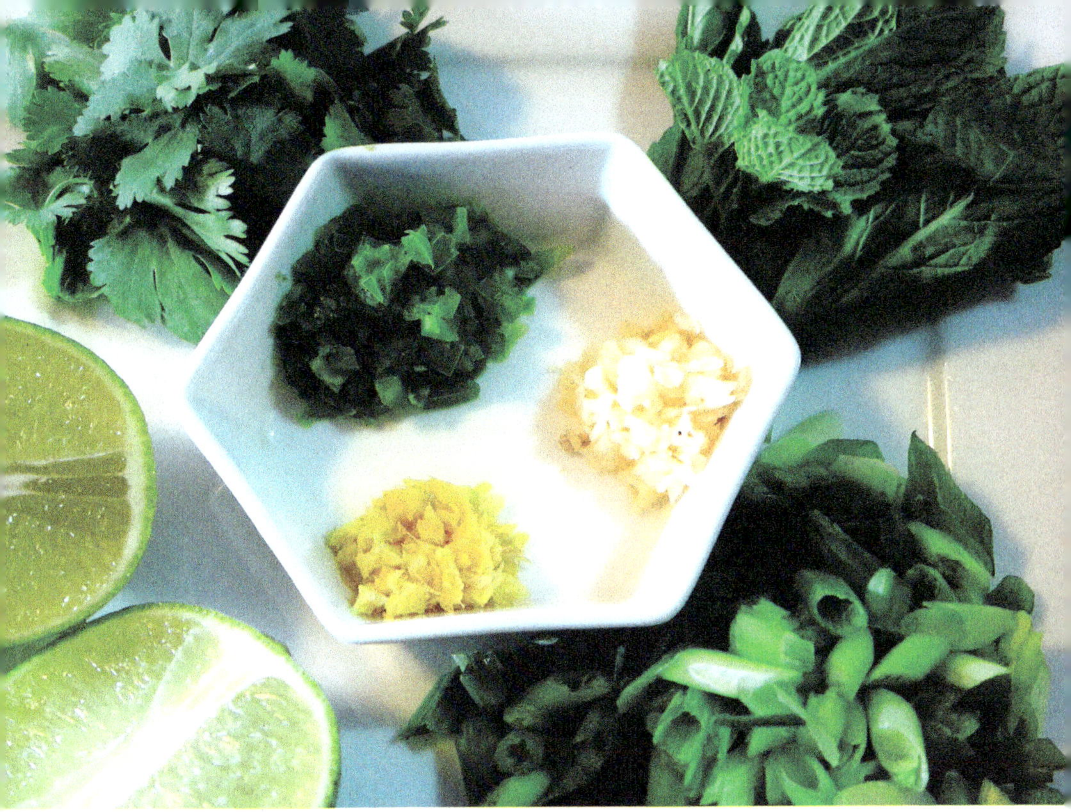

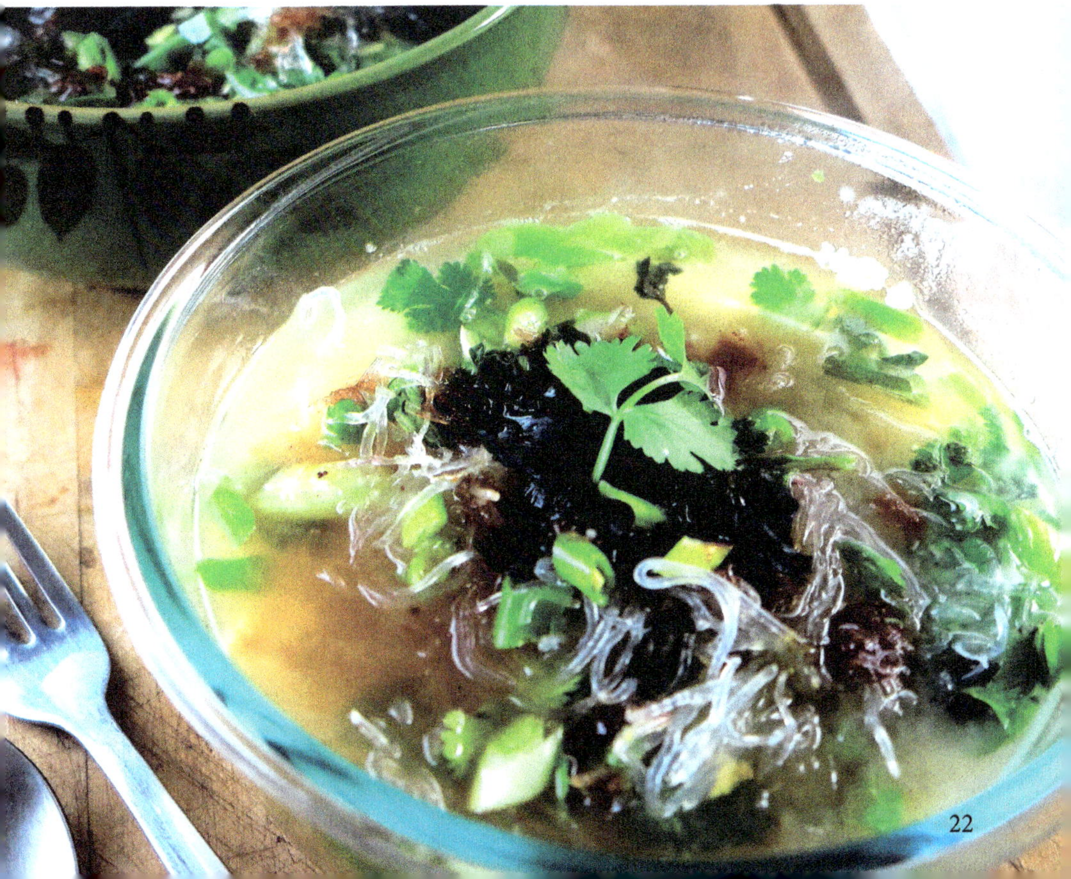

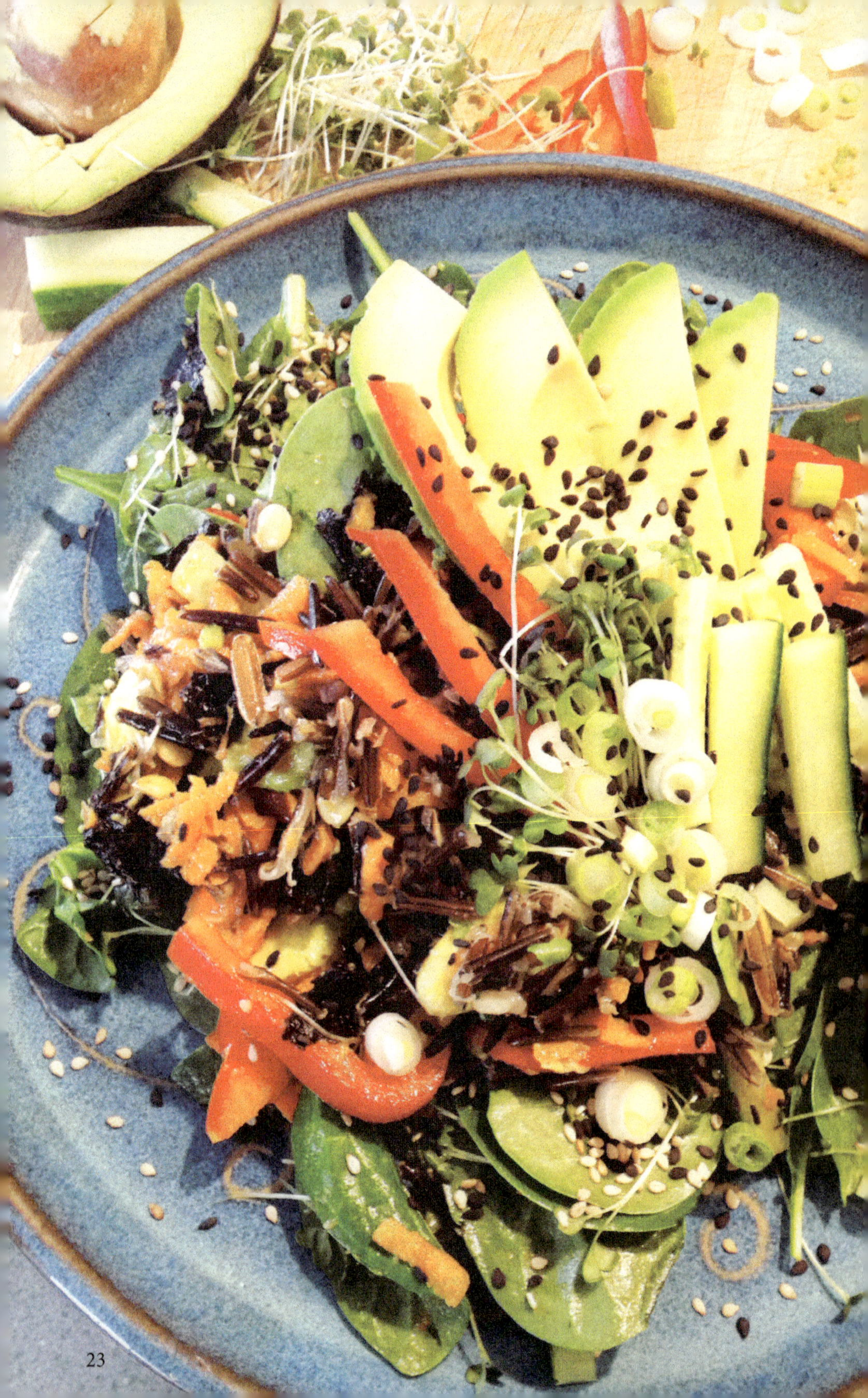

wasabi ginger sushi salad

THE SALAD:
2 AVOCADOS
1 CUP SPROUTED WILD RICE
2 CUPS SHREDDED CARROT
6 SHEETS OF NORI, TORN UP
1 CUCUMBER, JULIENNED
1 RED PEPPER, JULIENNED

BLACK AND WHITE SESAME SEEDS
MIXED BABY GREENS
MICROGREENS OR SPROUTS

INGREDIENTS - THE SAUCE:
½ CUP GF TAMARI
3 TBSP TOASTED SESAME OIL
3 TBSP WASABI POWDER
1 TBSP GINGER POWDER
1 TBSP FRESH GINGER
1 TBSP OLIVE OIL

Procedure:
Mix the sauce ingredients in a mason jar and shake vigorously. In a separate bowl, chop up the salad ingredients except the greens, add sauce to taste and mix with tongs. Sprinkle with sesame seeds and serve on a bed of mixed baby greens and/or sprouts. Refrigerate any leftover sauce and use within two weeks.

LOVE, THE SECRET INGREDIENT!

Doesn't food taste better when it's lovingly prepared?

This is one of my go-to salads and it's so delicious that I just had to include it within these pages. It always changes, yet there is a certain element that sticks no matter what ingredients are swapped and replaced. That's because it's always perfectly taste-balanced and infused with love. Putting love into our food preparation is a way of communicating without words. It is a conscious action that says, "I love you and I nourish you with life energy!" With a harmonious mix of sweet, salty, savoury, sour, fatty and even bitter flavours, this salad will make your heart and taste buds sing!

The concept of food combining has intrigued me for some time. In our stomach, sits the gurgling hydrochloric acid chock full of digestive enzymes ready to destroy the next morsel that falls in. But this powerful brew can only handle so much at a time. When we reach for the potatoes and miso gravy, our tummy will be ready. When we start adding everything but the kitchen sink on top, it becomes a little confused. Starches and proteins take different concentrations of hydrochloric acid, different unique enzymes and also different amounts of time to break down into the simple sugars that fuel our bodies and minds. If the starches get broken down first, the proteins pass through the stomach improperly digested and thus a slew of digestive issues from contaminated blood to decreased nutrient assimilation may occur. While proteins convert into amino acids during digestion, starches will have already started to ferment leaving you feel nauseous and bloated. Improper food combining over a long period of time may even cause degenerative health conditions.

For people with health challenges and digestive issues, eating as simply as possible will allow for better nutrient absorption and more energy to spend elsewhere. The good news is that basic food combining for better digestion and nutrient absorption is easy to implement into your day-to-day routine. You'll still have to be mindful of that home-cooked buffet at grandma's house, but if you follow these tips, your tummy will thank you. In the example of this yummy Italian Tomato Salad recipe, the simplicity of the ingredients within allows the potent phytonutrient, lycopene to be better absorbed when mixed with olive oil. With this specific combination, we increase the lycopene absorption exponentially.

TOP FOOD COMBINING TIPS FOR BETTER DIGESTION

1. Eat simple meals. Foods eaten alone or with one or two other foods will be the easiest to digest.

2. Eat dense proteins first. Since proteins need the most hydrochloric acid, it's best to give them a head start.

3. Don't combine starches and proteins – If you just can't give up beans and rice, certain spices such as ginger and cumin can help digest them together.

4. Greens such as kale, spinach and arugula as well as non-starchy vegetables such as carrots, broccoli and cabbage combine well with everything except dessert – which should be eaten alone.

5. Don't drink water with meals since it can dilute the digestive enzymes and hydrochloric acid, interfering with the natural digestive process. Drink water at least fifteen minutes before a meal or one hour after.

6. Eat fruits alone, especially watermelon. Fruit and other desserts with a high sugar content break down quickly. Let them do their thing before adding anything else. Otherwise you'll risk fermentation (the bad kind) in the gut that can cause toxic by-products such as lactic acid and even carbon dioxide. This is indigestion at its meanest. So go ahead and eat your dessert first!

italian tomato salad

INGREDIENTS:
2 CUPS CHOPPED ROMA TOMATOES
2 TBSP FRESH BASIL
1 TBSP FRESH OREGANO
1 CLOVE GARLIC, MINCED
DRIZZLE OF EXTRA-VIRGIN OLIVE OIL
PINCH OF PINK SALT
FRESHLY GROUND BLACK PEPPER

This traditional Italian salad is always a crowd pleaser and so simple to make! Use the extra-virgin olive oil and pink salt in moderation. Toss in a bowl and let flavours mingle for a few hours. This dish tastes great the next day too!

SAVE ROOM FOR SNACKING!

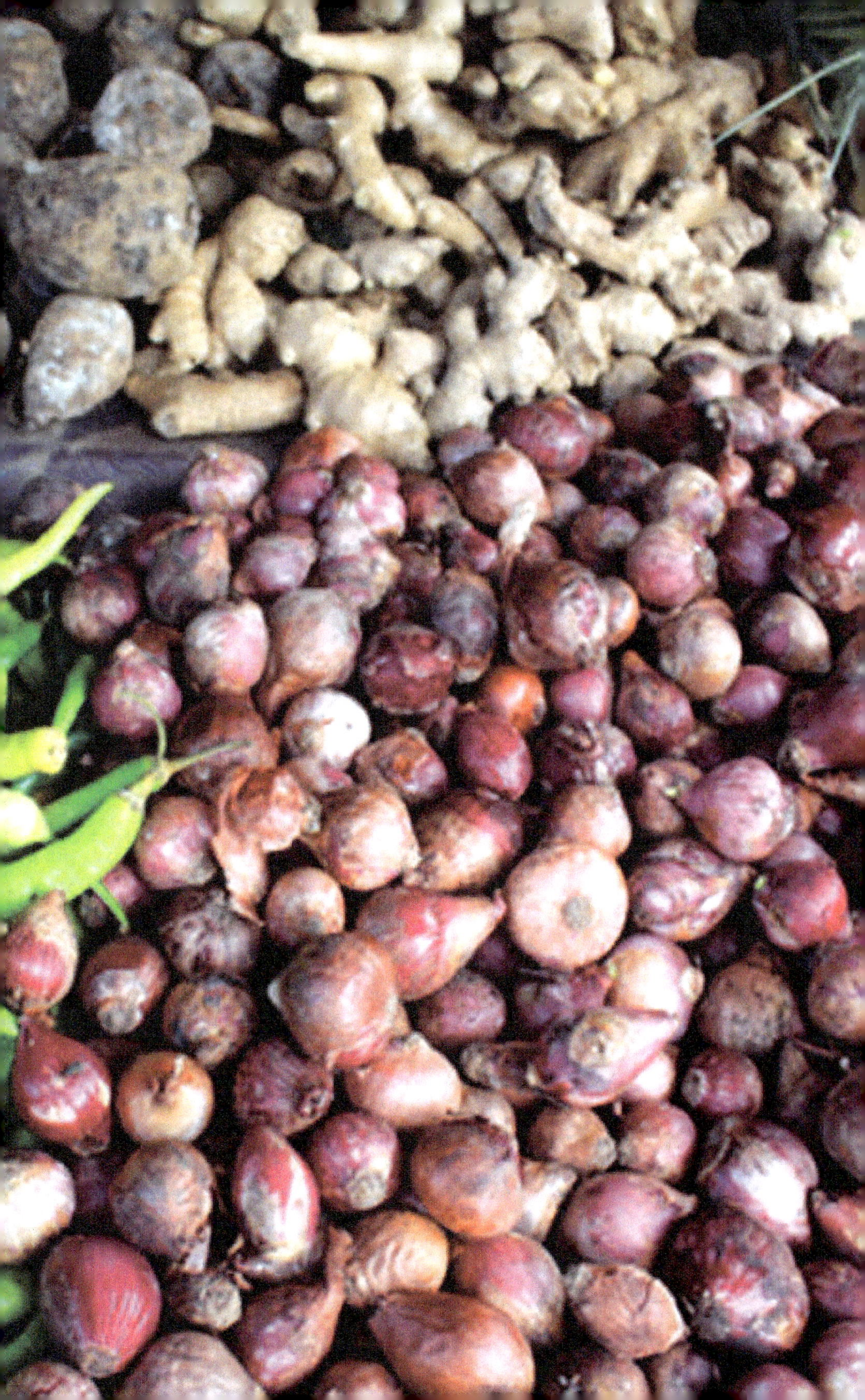

EAT A RAINBOW

By eating a variety of fruits and vegetables of all colours everyday, we can strengthen our immune system and potentially protect ourselves from chronic disease and pestering health conditions. Variety is key. If you eat the same food day in, day out, you will eventually develop a sensitivity. For example, eating spinach everyday can lead to a build up of oxalic acid and contribute to kidney stones. By mixing it up, we are getting a plethora of vitamins, minerals, essential fatty acids, electrolytes, phytonutrients and antioxidants, exactly what our bodies need to function at their optimal level.

This recipe is the base for a whole bunch of grawnola. Use your imagination and taste balance as you go. The amounts can vary and you may even want to omit ingredients or add others that are not listed in the recipe.

grawnola

Ingredients:

3 cups raw buckwheat groats
1 cup gluten-free oats
1 cup goji berries, soaked with ½ cup raisins
(be sure to save soaking water from the raisins and the gojis)
½ cup pumpkin seeds
½ cup hemp hearts
½ cup coconut shreds
¼ cup chia seeds
1 tbsp maca powder

2 medium apples, cored
2 bananas
2 tsp fresh grated ginger
2 tsp orange zest
½ cup soaking water from raisins and gojis
Add spices to your liking, including; cinnamon, cardamom or nutmeg

Procedure:
If you are using pre-sprouted buckwheat, skip the next paragraph.

If you are using raw buckwheat, be sure to soak it for at least six hours and rinse well. Leave it to sprout for two days or until little white tails start to show. During this time, be sure to rinse the sprouts a couple of times per day.

Once the buckwheat is sprouted, you can begin making the granola by pureeing the apples, bananas, water, ginger, orange and spices in a blender until it resembles apple sauce. Empty into a mixing bowl, add the rest of the ingredients and mix well. Spread mixture on a Teflex sheet and dehydrate eight to twelve hours. Break the mixture up into clumps and dehydrate for another four hours, or until completely dry. Once dry store in an airtight container. Serve with fresh Brazil nut mylk (recipe on page 88).

SOAKING NUTS AND SEEDS? SAVE SOME TIME

When you see nuts and seeds that need to be "soaked and rinsed", you'll want to soak overnight in most cases, especially bigger nuts like cashews. Smaller seeds like sesame take only a few hours. If you purchase pre-sprouted nuts and seeds, you can eliminate a big step in the process of many of the recipes in this book. When I get busy and don't have the foresight to plan my soaking and sprouting, I order pre-sprouted seeds and nuts from realrawfood.com, a small Canadian, family-run business that is dedicated to quality, organic and fair-trade bulk foods. If you don't live in Canada, there are many reputable sources online and your local health food store may have some in stock or be able to point you in the right direction.

the crust

INGREDIENTS:
2 CUPS CHOPPED CARROTS
2 MEDIUM ONIONS, CHOPPED
2 CUPS SOAKED SUNFLOWER SEEDS
1 ¼ CUP DRIED SPROUTED BUCKWHEAT
1 CUP GROUND FLAX SEED
1 CUP SUNDRIED TOMATOES (SOAKED 2+ HOURS)
¼ CUP FRESH PARSLEY, MINCED
¼ CUP COLD PRESSED OLIVE OIL
2 TSP ITALIAN HERB BLEND
1 TSP PINK SALT
2 DROPS EACH BLACK PEPPER ESSENTIAL OIL (OPTIONAL)

Procedure:
Place carrot, onion, sundried tomatoes and spices in the food processor, process until smooth. Drain and rinse buckwheat and sunflower seeds, add to the processor, continue to process until well combined, place mixture in mixing bowl and stir in ground flax. Place batter on three Teflex sheets and distribute evenly. Score an "x" then a "+" into the batter to form eight triangles. Dehydrate at 118 °F for twelve hours, Once the top is dry, flip, remove Teflex and dehydrate for another twelve hours or more on mesh screens, depending on thickness of crust. In an air-tight container, these will last for months - if you can save them that is.

pickled onion

INGREDIENTS:
½ CUP OF SLICED RED ONION
½ CUP LIME JUICE
A PINCH OF PINK SALT

Procedure:
Marinate in a glass mason jar for at least two hours; then it's ready to eat and can be stored in the fridge for a week. This is how it is done in Mexico!

Pizza assembly:
pizza crust, black pepper truffle cashew cream (see recipe on page 39), zesty tomato sauce, cilantro pesto and pickled onion.
Top with: kalamata olives, fresh cucumber slices, broccoli sprouts, baby kale or freshly sliced pears!

cilantro pesto

rawkin' raw pizza

INGREDIENTS:
3 CUPS FRESH CILANTRO
1 CUP SPINACH OR KALE
½ CUP CASHEWS
  (OR SUNFLOWER SEEDS FOR NUT-FREE CUISINE)
¼ CUP OLIVE OIL
1 CLOVE GARLIC
3 TBSP LEMON JUICE
¼ TSP PINK SALT

Procedure:
Pulse in a food processor until chunky, but well mixed.

zesty tomato sauce

INGREDIENTS:
2 MEDIUM TOMATOES
1 CUP SUNDRIED TOMATOES (SOAKED TWO HOURS)
¼ CUP ONION
1 GARLIC CLOVE
1 SPRIG OF FRESH OREGANO
1 TBSP FRESH LEMON JUICE
1 TSP LEMON ZEST
2 MEDJOOL DATES
4 KALAMATA OLIVES, PITTED
A PINCH OF PINK SALT AND CAYENNE PEPPER

Procedure:
Combine all ingredients in a food processor and pulse until everything is well mixed, but still a little chunky.

basil kalamata tapenade

INGREDIENTS:
¾ CUP ALMONDS
½ CUP PINE NUTS
1 CUP KALAMATA OLIVES, PITTED
3 CUPS FRESH BASIL
1 CUP SUNDRIED TOMATOES (SOAKED IN WATER FOR 2-4 HOURS)
¼ CUP OLIVE OIL
1 CLOVE GARLIC
1 TBSP LEMON JUICE
1 TBSP FRESH OREGANO
PINCH OF SALT

THIS TASTES SUPER YUM ON THE RAW PIZZA CRUST TOO!

Procedure for the tapenade and relish:
Add ingredients to the food processor, pulse until blended but not homogenized.

pear lemongrass salsa

INGREDIENTS:
2 ASIAN PEAR, SMALL DICE
½ CUP RED ONION, MINCED
1 SERRANO PEPPER, MINCED, SEEDS REMOVED
2 STALKS OF FRESH MINCED LEMONGRASS
HANDFUL OF FRESH CILANTRO LEAVES, CHOPPED FINELY
A TBSP OF EACH:
OLIVE OIL, LIME JUICE, LIQUID SWEETENER, APPLE CIDER VINEGAR
PINCH OF SALT

Procedure:
Combine salsa ingredients in a bowl and enjoy fresh!

curried goji berry relish

Ingredients:
½ cup dried cranberries
1 red pepper
2 dates, soaked and pitted
3 garlic cloves, chopped
¼ cup goji berries
2 tbsp olive oil
1 tbsp orange zest or 2 drops of wild orange oil
2 tsp curry powder
pinch salt and black pepper

lentil dippers

Ingredients:
2 cups carrots
1 cup sprouted lentils
2 cups sprouted sunflower seeds
¾ cup orange juice
¼ cup onion
¼ cup olive oil
1 tbsp liquid sweetener
½ tbsp curry powder
½ tbsp poultry seasoning
1 tsp medicinal mushroom powder
½ tsp pink salt

Procedure:
Process the carrots in a food processor until diced. Add in all of the other ingredients and process until well blended. Shape onto oblong pieces and arrange on Teflex sheets, which fit on top of a mesh dehydrator screen. Dehydrate at 115° for 10 hours and flip half way. Serve with curry mango mustard.

curry mango mustard

INGREDIENTS:
½ CUP YOUNG THAI COCONUT
½ CUP FROZEN MANGO (THAWED)
2 TBSP DIJON MUSTARD
1 TBSP APPLE CIDER VINEGAR
1 TBSP COCONUT NECTAR/MAPLE SYRUP/RAW HONEY
2 TSP GINGER
¼ INCH FRESH TURMERIC
1 TSP GARAM MASALA
PINCH OF CAYENNE AND PINK SALT

Procedure:
Add ingredients to a high-speed blender, blend until smooth. Dip lentil dippers and enjoy thoroughly!

TURMERIC ~ ANTI-INFLAMMATORY MAGIC

Turmeric has long been used as a powerful anti-inflammatory in both Chinese and Indian medicinal practices. It is a warming spice, good for the cold weather blues when added to anything. Sweet or savoury, it's not just for curry. Applied topically, it can prevent infection in cuts and scrapes, soothe toothaches and heal bruises. If eaten, say goodbye to flatulence and even painful menstruation. The active oil in turmeric is called "curcumin" and produces no toxicity – so you can consume it every day. In many cases, a daily dose of turmeric has helped people reduce symptoms of rheumatoid arthritis, IBS. It may even prevent cancer due to curcumin's antioxidant effects that enable it to protect our cells from free radicals that can damage cellular DNA.

pesto portobello mushrooms

INGREDIENTS:
2 CUPS WALNUTS
¼ CUP PINE NUTS
6 CUPS PACKED BASIL LEAVES
2 CUPS KALE, CHOPPED
2 CUPS ZUCCHINI, CHOPPED
½ CUP EXTRA-VIRGIN OLIVE OIL
½ CUP NUTRITIONAL YEAST
¼ CUP LEMON JUICE
¼ CUP OF MISO
4 CLOVES GARLIC, CHOPPED
1 TSP MEDICINAL MUSHROOM POWDER
FRESH-CRACKED BLACK PEPPER

CHERRY TOMATOES FOR GARNISH
6 PORTOBELLO MUSHROOMS

Procedure:
Combine all the above in a food processor and pulse until well mixed. Rinse Portobello mushrooms, pat dry with paper towel and cut out the stem. You can save these for something else later, a pâté perhaps! Fill generously with the pesto, cut cherry tomatoes in half and press into the pesto. Place on mesh screens, cover with an upside-down bowl and dehydrate for four hours at 145 °F. They should be soft, juicy and warm by this time! Serve immediately.

You can easily make this recipe nut-free by substituting the walnuts and pine nuts for sunflower and pumpkin seeds.

Medicinal Mushrooms and Immunity

From the ancient Chinese to the Pharaohs in Egypt, medicinal mushrooms have been long used and revered for their health benefits. Maitake, reishi, chaga, cordyceps, coriolus and shiitake are all considered medicinal mushrooms. Touted as super immune boosting fungi, having both polyphenols and long-chain polysaccharides - these mushrooms have been proven to enhance immune response. Due to their high antioxidant activity, by consuming a wide variety of these different mushroom species, you can protect your DNA from oxidative stress. If you're feeling under the weather, reach for a blend of medicinal mushrooms in powder form and add them to everything: smoothies, dressings, lattes and salads.

38

black pepper truffle cashew cream

INGREDIENTS:
1 CUP RAW CASHEWS, SOAKED OVERNIGHT AND RINSED
(YOU CAN ALSO TRY PUMPKIN OR SUNFLOWER SEEDS
FOR A NUT-FREE OPTION)
½ CUP SAUERKRAUT JUICE (SPEEDS UP THE FERMENTATION PROCESS)
2 TBSP NUTRITIONAL YEAST
1 TBSP TRUFFLE OIL
½ TSP ONION POWDER
1 TSP PINK SALT
1 DROP BLACK PEPPER ESSENTIAL OIL (OPTIONAL)

CRUSHED PEPPERCORNS FOR GARNISH

EXPERIMENT WITH THIS RECIPE, TRY ADDING A DRIZZLE OF HERBES-INFUSED OLIVE OIL AND A TBSP OF HERBS DE PROVENCE. AMAZING!

Procedure:
There are two ways to make this amazing spread. You can put in the effort to make a cashew cream roll that is ready to slice or simply make a dip. The roll will definitely impress, but the quick dip can be made in half the time.

The dip: Blend all ingredients except peppercorns until very smooth. Scoop out into a bowl, dust with pepper and serve immediately with Kale Curry Crackers (see recipe on page 50).

The roll: Place a large strainer over a bowl and line with a triple layer of cheesecloth. Spoon the cashew mixture into the cheesecloth. Fold the sides of the cloth over the cashew mixture and gently roll it into an oval shape. Twist ends of the cloth and secure with elastic bands. Let stand twenty-four hours at room temperature. It will ferment, thus enhancing the probiotic count and giving it a tangy flavour. The next day, unroll cashew log and roll in crushed peppercorns. Place in the dehydrator for twenty hours and turn periodically. It is ready when you can pick it up with two hands and it seems reasonably solid to slice.

cauliflower mash

Ingredients:

2 heads cauliflower, chopped into small pieces
1 cup pine nuts
6 tbsp miso paste
3 garlic cloves, minced
½ cup olive oil
Fresh ground black pepper to taste
¼ cup chopped parsley (mix in by hand)

Garnish with chopped celery
pea shoots/sprouts
fresh dill
sweet and smoky coconut chips
smoked paprika to sprinkle on top

Procedure:
Place all (except parsley) in a food processor until well mixed and chunky or continue to process until as creamy as you like them. Transfer to bowl and mix in parsley by hand.

tahini gravy

Ingredients:
1 cup water
¼ cup tahini
¼ cup chick pea miso
¼ cup nutritional yeast
2 tbsp gf tamari
1 tbsp fresh green onion
1 tbsp dijon mustard

Procedure:
Blend in a high-speed blender until creamy.

sweet and smoky coconut chips

3 cups coconut flakes
2 tbsp maple syrup
2 tbsp gf tamari
1 tbsp extra-virgin olive oil
2 tsp liquid smoke (hickory)
1 tsp pink salt
pinch of chili powder

This recipe may taste like the 'b' word, but I assure you, no little piggies were harmed in the makin' of this bacon!

Procedure:
Toss together in a large mixing bowl and then dehydrate on Teflex sheets at 118 °F for four hours. Remove Teflex sheets and continue to dehydrate for four more hours until crispy. Store extras in a glass jar and add to everything! Both sweet and savoury dishes will sing with flavour! Try this recipe with thinly sliced eggplant or zucchini instead of coconut for another crispy alternative!

savoury sage and pecan medley

INGREDIENTS:
4 CUPS ZUCCHINI, DICED
2 APPLES, DICED
2 CUPS CELERY, DICED
1 CUP RED CABBAGE, CHIFFONADE
¾ CUP ONION, DICED FINE
½ CUP WALNUTS, ROUGHLY CHOPPED
½ CUP PUMPKIN SEEDS
½ CUP DRIED CRANBERRIES
¼ CUP EXTRA-VIRGIN OLIVE OIL
2 TBSP GF TAMARI
1 TBSP CELERY SALT
1 TBSP SAGE POWDER
2 TSP FRESH THYME
1 TSP MEDICINAL MUSHROOM POWDER
2 DROPS ROSEMARY OIL
PINCH OF PINK SALT

SERVE ON A BED OF ROMAINE LETTUCE, CHIFFONADE

Procedure:
Add all ingredients to a big bowl, toss together and let marinate for two to four hours. You may dehydrate at 118°F for four hours (without the romaine), until warm or eat straight away stuffed in romaine leaves. I think this is my favourite dish. I've made it so many times, so many different ways.

Nut-Free Plant-Based Cuisine

Even though a lot of the recipes within these pages call for nuts of some kind, there are many other alternatives if you are allergic or if your preference is to avoid them. Depending on your original recipe, the following list will give you many ideas! Sometimes you can even take out the nuts altogether, like in the Savoury Sage and Pecan Medley. It is just as delicious without the pecans!

Savoury substitutions ~ sunflower seeds, pumpkin seeds, sesame seeds, tahini, mushrooms, celery, any root vegetable (beet, parsnip, carrot), olives, oatmeal, avocado.

Sweet substitutions ~ sunflower seeds, sesame seeds, tahini, cacao nibs, oats, coconut meat, coconut butter and coconut flour. Despite the name, most people with nut allergies can eat coconut. Young coconut is also a great substitute for any dessert calling for cashews.

THE HEALTH BENEFITS OF SEAWEED ~
THE GREAT GRANDMOTHER OF ALL SUPERFOODS!

Seaweed is nature's ancient superfood and the secret to our ancestors' health and longevity for over 2000 years. Because of its high content of naturally occurring iodine, it balances and strengthens our thyroid function. Seaweed is also found to be an abundant resource for trace minerals necessary for our bodies to maintain healthy functions. It contains minerals such as chromium, zinc, calcium, magnesium, manganese, potassium and iron. It is also rich in essential fatty acids (EFA's) and antioxidants and is an excellent source of chlorophyll, the life blood of the plant and interestingly, only one molecule different from human blood. Studies indicated algae varieties, including spirulina and chlorella can help clear the body from radiation. Radiation negatively affects the brain, heart, GI tract, and the reproductive and circulatory systems. Another perk is that the harvesting of seaweed and algae is sustainable without destroying its ecosystem.

The term seaweed encompasses a variety of types of algae and marine plants. It must be known that there are different species, with distinct flavors and nutrient contents. Below is a list of just some of the seaweeds used in this book.

Nori - The mainstream seaweed, nori has become a household name, thanks to miso soup and sushi. Often dried or toasted into sheets, it has ten times more calcium than milk.
Dulse - Reddish brown and may resemble a jerky. It is usually ground and sprinkled on salads and soups. It is nutrient-dense with vitamins, minerals, protein and antioxidants.
Kelp - One way of consuming kelp is by purchasing kelp noodles, a perfect substitute for pasta and noodle soup dishes which requires no cooking and takes on the flavour of any sauce.
Marine phytoplankton - My favourite all-around, great grandmother superfood of all. I use the fresh stuff in bottles. Add a squirt to your water, salad dressings and sauces for a boost of healthy omega 3 fatty acids like DHA and EPA - you don't have to guzzle cod liver oil anymore. Skip the middle man and go straight to the original source!

save the sea pâté

INGREDIENTS:
2 CUPS ALMONDS
2 TBSP GROUND FLAX SEEDS
2 TBSP HEMP OIL
5 CARROTS, CHOPPED
¼ CUP YELLOW ONION, CHOPPED
2 STALKS CELERY, CHOPPED
2 GARLIC CLOVES, MINCED
HALF A THUMB OF GINGER, MINCED
¼ CUP LEMON JUICE
2 TBSP GF TAMARI
2 TBSP DULSE

"the pâté formula"

INGREDIENTS:
2 CUPS NUTS OR SEEDS (SUNFLOWER SEEDS, SESAME SEEDS, WALNUTS, ALMONDS, PECANS, CASHEWS, PUMPKIN SEEDS)
½ CUP FRESH HERBS (CILANTRO, BASIL, DILL, OREGANO, PARSLEY)
CHOOSE 2 VEGETABLES, ADD ½ CUP OF EACH (RED PEPPER, ZUCCHINI, BROCCOLI, CAULIFLOWER, GREEN PEAS, GREEN BEANS)
1 CUP ROOT VEGETABLE (CARROT, BEET, PARSNIP, YAM)
¼ CUP SOUR LIQUID (APPLE CIDER VINEGAR, LEMON OR LIME JUICE)
3 TBSP GROUND FLAX SEEDS OR CHIA SEEDS
2 TBSP OIL (OLIVE, HEMP, FLAX)
2 TBSP GF TAMARI

rawkin' rollies

Procedure for the pâté:
Process the harder vegetables first then add the rest of the ingredients and process until smooth and creamy. Taste as you go - you may want to add more gluten-free (gf) tamari (umami), extra-virgin olive oil (fat) or lemon juice (sour).

Assembly: Lay your nori roll on the cutting board, spread the pâté on half of the nori and lay baby greens, fresh sprouts and julienned red pepper, cucumber and avocado in the middle of the pâté. Paint a little lemon juice on the end of the nori that is not covered in pâté with your fingers and roll tightly, sealing together the ends as you do. Cut into pieces with a sharp knife, sawing gently so as not to squish the roll. Dip in the Sushi Salad Sauce on page 24. Delicious!

kale curry crackers

Ingredients:
- 2 cups sunflower seeds
- 2 cups chopped carrots
- 1 cup kale
- 1 cup ground flax seed
- ½ cup onion
- 2 tbsp gf tamari
- 1 tbsp olive oil
- 1 tbsp lemon juice
- 2 tsp curry powder

Procedure:
In a food processor, process all ingredients into a smooth batter. Spread the batter a quarter-inch thick onto dehydrator trays with nonstick sheets. Score the batter with a spatula into square shapes. Start dehydrating at 145°F. After two hours, turn the dehydrator down to 110°F. After four hours or until the batter doesn't stick to the Teflex, flip the crackers and remove the nonstick sheet. Continue dehydrating for an additional eigth to twelvehours until crispy. These crispy yummies can be stored in a cool, dark place for weeks in an airtight container.

the "cracker" formula

INGREDIENTS:
2 CUPS NUTS/SEEDS
1 CUP ROOT VEGETABLE
1 CUP LEAFY GREEN
1 CUP GROUND OR WHOLE FLAX/CHIA SEEDS
½ CUP ONION/LEEK
1 TBSP OLIVE OIL
1 TBSP LEMON JUICE
FRESH SPICES AND HERBS AS DESIRED
A PINCH OF SALT/DULSE/CELERY SALT AS DESIRED (TASTE BALANCE)

Procedure:
Follow the same procedure as the Kale Curry Crackers

SOAKING AND SPROUTING

Sprouts are an excellent source of nutrients. When sprouted, legumes and other seeds are crunchy and fresh, adding a wide array of vitamins and minerals to your diet. Dried seeds and legumes are incomplete proteins but when sprouted, they have an increase in all nine essential amino acids, thus up-ing the protein factor too. Imagine eating the combined nutrition of a thousand baby plants! When you eat sprouts, this is exactly what you are doing. You'll also have more food. One cup of dry lentils equals four cups of sprouted lentils after only a few days.

To sprout at home, you'll need viable seeds, a mason jar, mesh screen, a rubber band and some water. In the jar, soak the seeds in room-temp water overnight. The next day, rinse and hang upside-down to drain through a mesh screen, after securing the screen with a rubber band so the seeds don't fall out. You can also use a proper sprouting tray made for sprouting. This is actually easier. Each seed has a different soaking and sprouting time. All require rinsing at least twice daily and a cool place to drain fully. Leave the sprouts to grow out of direct sunlight. Upon harvest time, place them in the sun for a few hours and through the miracle of photosynthesis, the little yellow leaves will turn bright green! Generally, all sprouts can be eaten when their sprout tails are twice as long as the seed itself - but some can grow much longer. The following list is not extensive, but includes sprouting and harvesting times for seeds, grains and legumes in this book.

Lucky us! Sprouts go with everything! Top on everything that goes in your mouth: soups, salads, cooked dishes and veggies. You can even add them to smoothies!

	soak	harvest
Alfalfa, Broccoli	overnight	5 days
Wild Rice	36 hours	4 days
Lentils	24 hours	3 days
Garbanzo	36 hours	3 days
Buckwheat	15 hours	2 days
Almonds	24 hours	1 day
Sunflower Seeds	12 hours	1 day
Pumpkin Seeds	12 hours	1 day
Walnuts	overnight	-
Cashews	3 hours	-

Fermented Food: Good for Gut Health

The process of fermentation begins when decay consumes one form and new life in the form of millions of microscopic interactions and processes takes over. Complex organic molecules begin to breakdown and form smaller, more digestible organisms. The microscopic wizardry happens as bacteria and fungi, yeasts and moulds do their thing, an absolutely essential process in the complex cycle of life. With the addition of pink salt and the air barrier created by the brine, harmful bacteria are kept at bay. This also creates the right conditions for beneficial bacteria like lactobacilli to thrive. When we eat food that has been fermented, these microorganisms help us digest efficiently and stimulate our immune system to function as it should. Fermented foods also help kill the stubborn yeasts that lead to Candidiasis.

While discovering the Western world, Captain Cook knew the benefits of fermentation. He and his crew evaded scurvy thanks to its high amount of vitamin C in the barrels upon barrels of sauerkraut they kept on board. In Korea today, kimchi is on the table at every meal and tempeh, originating in Java, is still one of Indonesia's staple sources of protein. If fermented foods can be made with limited resources, as it was back then, certainly we can brew up a multitude of fermented magic in our own kitchens.

My intention is to inspire you to experiment for yourself. With a little patience and effort, you'll discover what has been common knowledge for millennia; the way to build a healthy army of intestinal flora is to boost your immunity and improve your digestion in your very own kitchens. With just a spoonful of kraut a day, you'll do wonders for your immunity!

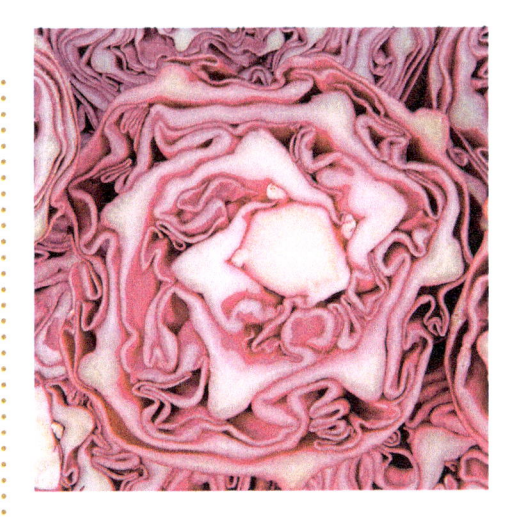

Miso, tempeh, natto, sauerkraut, kimchi, kombucha, kefir and home-made yogurts all have naturally occurring pro-biotics!

basic kraut

Ingredients:
2 1/4 kilos of cabbage and or
mixed root vegetables
3 tbsp of pink salt

SALT?
Whenever you see "pinch of pink salt" in this book, I am referring to Himalayan pink salt. With 98 trace minerals, it's the best salt of them all.

51

Time frame: One to four weeks (more pink salt, more time)
Special Equipment: Ceramic crock with fitted weights or 1-litre, wide-mouth mason jar (for the kraut), 250 ml mason jar, filled with water (as the weight or use a boiled, scrubbed rock in a Ziploc)

bold brassica kraut

INGREDIENTS:
BASIC KRAUT WITH BROCCOLI,
CAULIFLOWER AND KALE
ADD A PINCH OF CUMIN SEEDS AT EACH LAYER

korean kimchi

INGREDIENTS:
BASIC KRAUT WITH 2 TBSP FRESH GRATED GINGER, 2 TBSP
MINCED GARLIC, 2 TBSP RED PEPPER FLAKES

Procedure:
Thinly slice the cabbage/veggies (leave a few large leaves for the top layer). Layer the cabbage and veggies, adding a pinch of pink salt (and spices) to each layer as you go. You must then punch/press the cabbage or pound it with a pestle after each layer in order to get the culturing process started. When combined with pink salt, the water of the cabbage will be drawn out and become the brine. When ready to cover, arrange whole cabbage leaves over the top and make sure it is totally covered. You must then weigh the kraut down with either a boiled, scrubbed rock in a Ziploc or if you are using a traditional crock pot, it will come with the weights. This prevents the cabbage from floating and keeps it under the brine. Do not seal the jar. As contents ferment, carbon dioxide will build up and need somewhere to escape.

Over the first twenty-four hours, check the kraut three to four times and press it down to make sure that the brine level rises to just above the cabbage. If after twenty-four hours there isn't enough brine to completely cover the cabbage, dissolve a tablespoon of pink salt in 1 cup of water and use this brine to fill in the water line to just above the level of the cabbage.

Depending on the temperature of your kitchen, and the humidity of your climate, the sauerkraut will take anywhere from a week or more to ferment and reach that tangy flavor. I usually leave it for four weeks. You don't have to check it until you are ready to eat it. You may see a white/greyish mold on top, this is normal but remove most of it before eating. To package the kraut, transfer it to a mason jar and store in the fridge. It will keep for months.

luscious lemon cream cake ~ page 56

Delicious Desserts

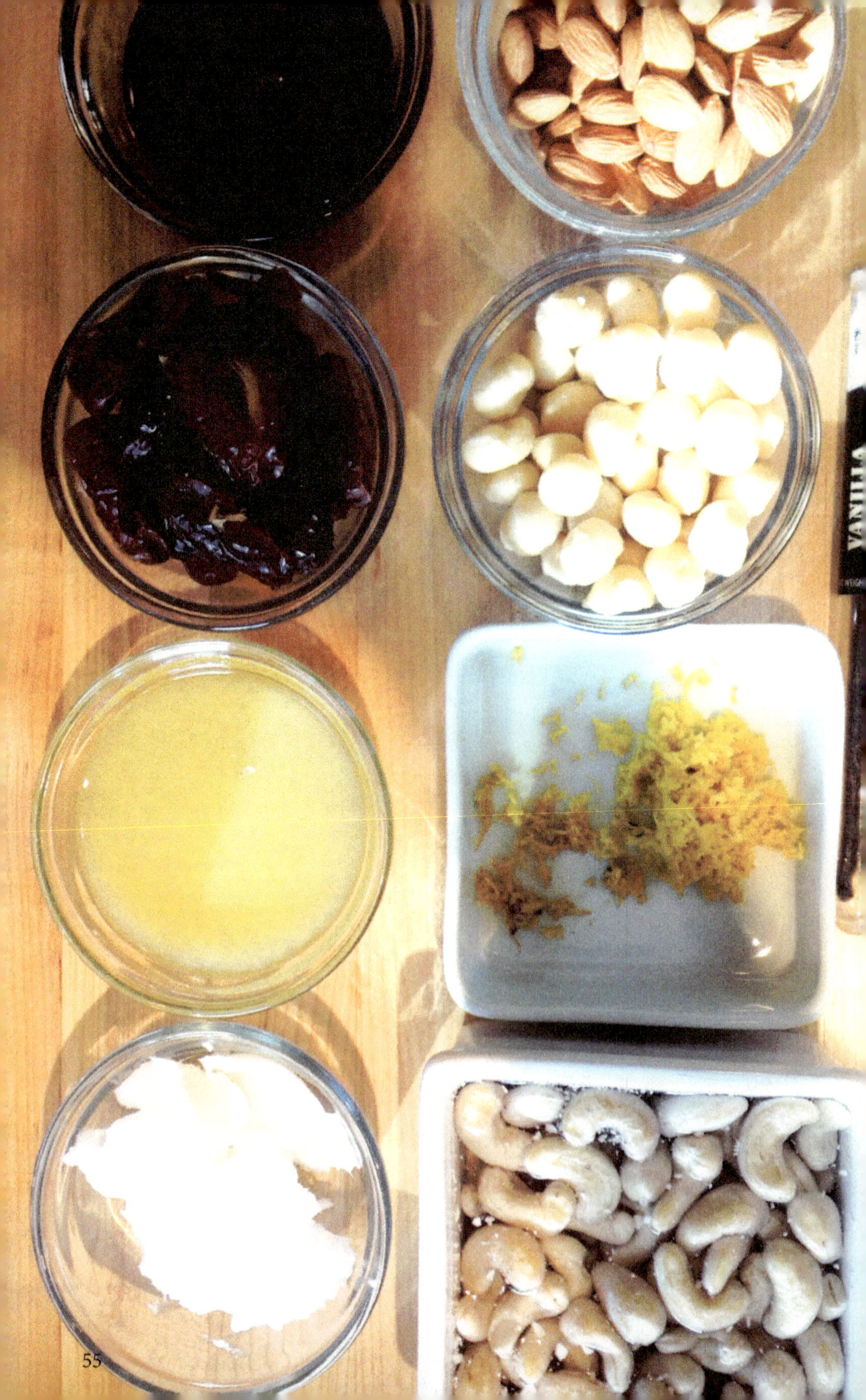
VANILLA

luscious lemon cream cake

CRUST:
½ CUP ALMONDS
½ CUP MACADAMIA NUTS
¼ CUP MEDJOOL DATES
¼ CUP COCONUT SHREDS
2 TBSP COCONUT OIL, WARMED TO LIQUID IN THE DEHYDRATOR
PINCH OF VANILLA POWDER
PINCH OF PINK SALT

Procedure: First pulse the nuts then add the rest of the ingredients to the food processor. Pulse until well combined.

FILLING:
1 ½ CUPS CASHEWS , SOAKED AND RINSED
½ CUP FRESH LEMON JUICE
ZEST OF ONE LEMON
2 TBSP COCONUT OIL, WARMED TO LIQUID IN THE DEHYDRATOR
½ CUP YOUNG THAI COCONUT MEAT
3 TBSP LIQUID SWEETENER
PINCH OF PINK SALT

TOPPING:
½ CUP MANGO
1 TBSP LEMON JUICE
½ TBSP PSYLLIUM HUSK POWDER

Procedure: Blend in a high-speed blender. Don't be afraid to get tough with it. This is the secret to the creamy consistency.

Assembly:
Sprinkle a little bit of loose coconut flakes on the bottom of a spring-form pan (about six inches in diameter) then press the crust mixture into the pan. While preparing the filling, place the crust into the freezer to set. Once the filling acheives a creamy texture while blending, pour into pan using a spatula to smooth the surface. Place entire cake in freezer to set (at least three hours). Take out half an hour before serving to thaw slightly. Garnish with lemon zest and mango topping.

mason jar maca carrot cake with lemony vanilla frosting

INGREDIENTS - CARROT CAKE:
1 ½ CUPS OATS
4 LARGE CARROTS, PEELED AND CHOPPED INTO SMALL CHUNKS
½ CUP PECANS
½ CUP DRIED COCONUT
1 TBSP MACA POWDER
1 TBSP LIQUID SWEETENER
2 TSP CINNAMON
½ TSP NUTMEG
1 CUP SOAKED RAISINS (MIX IN BY HAND)

Procedure for the cake:
Combine all ingredients, except raisins in the food processor and process until it all begins to stick together. Mix in raisins by hand.

INGREDIENTS - LEMONY VANILLA FROSTING:
1 ½ CUPS CASHEWS (SOAKED)
¼ CUP YOUNG THAI COCONUT
¼ CUP LIQUID SWEETENER
2 TBSP COCONUT OIL, WARMED TO A LIQUID IN DEHYDRATOR
2 TBSP LEMON JUICE
1 TBSP MACA POWDER
2 TSP VANILLA POWDER
2 TSP LEMON ZEST
1 TSP CAMU CAMU POWDER
2 DROPS LEMON ESSENTIAL OIL (OPTIONAL)
¼ CUP WATER

Procedure for the frosting:
Blend all ingredients in your high-speed blender until smooth, aerate when necessary.

Assembly:
Layer the cake and the frosting one after the other in a mason jar and garnish with crushed pecans, sliced carrot and cinnamon. For a neater looking cake, freeze after each layer and press firmly. Make a whole bunch and you've got dessert to go for a week!

IF EATEN AS A BREAKFAST, YOU'RE GOOD TO GO. IF EATEN AS DESSERT, ADD TWO SOAKED MEDJOOL DATES TO THE CAKE MIX

Maca ~ The Magic Adaptogenic Superfood of the Andes

Hailing from the Peruvian Andes of South America, maca is one of the highest altitude crops in the world, growing at around 4300 metres. Since it grows in extreme conditions, it is good for people who push their bodies to the maximum. Whether you are an athlete, live in a variable climate, or need to cope with the stress of modern life, maca can benefit you in many ways. Maca is an adaptogen, which allows our bodies to adapt to stress by increasing our blood-oxygen content, thus producing a normalizing effect called homeostasis - our bodies in perfect balance. It also supports the endocrine system, having positive effects on your adrenal hormones and it can repair exhausted adrenal glands. Maca also has aphrodisiac qualities and has been touted to increase libido for many centuries. The Incans knew of maca's ability to prolong energy and stamina. They even used it as an Incan currency in pre and post-Spanish conquest times. High in minerals such as calcium, copper, iodine, iron, magnesium, phosphorus, potassium, selenium, sulfur, tin and zinc, maca's versatility and untold health benefits make it one of the most powerful superfoods in the world.

The sad news is that in 2015 the price of maca skyrocketed as Chinese investors purchased maca fields in Peru. They also developed several patents for GMO maca, which they now grow in China. For many people, the consumption of maca as part of a healthy superfood diet may becoming a thing of the past. But if you are inclined to pay the high prices, beware of adulterated maca and only buy organically grown and pure.

chocolate almond pie

INGREDIENTS:
BOTTOM LAYER -
1 CUP ALMONDS, SOAKED AND RINSED
½ CUP DATES, PITTED
¼ CUP SHREDDED COCONUT
2 TBSP COCONUT OIL, WARMED TO LIQUID IN THE DEHYDRATOR
½ TSP VANILLA POWDER
PINCH OF PINK SALT

Procedure:
Using a food processor, mix until a dough-like ball forms. Press into a spring-form pan and place in the freezer while you prepare the cream topping.

INGREDIENTS:
TOP LAYER -
1 RIPE BANANA
½ CUP CASHEWS, SOAKED AND RINSED
½ CUP YOUNG THAI COCONUT
3 TBSP MAPLE SYRUP
½ CUP CACAO
1 TBSP COCONUT OIL, WARMED TO LIQUID IN THE DEHYDRATOR
2 TSP ALMOND ESSENTIAL OIL (OPTIONAL)

CACAO NIBS AND STRAWBERRIES FOR GARNISH

Procedure:
Blend in a high-speed blender until smooth. Aerate as necessary. Spread evenly on top of the bottom layer and place back in the freezer to set. Remove half an hour before serving. Slice and garnish with cacao nibs and organic strawberries.
Yum!

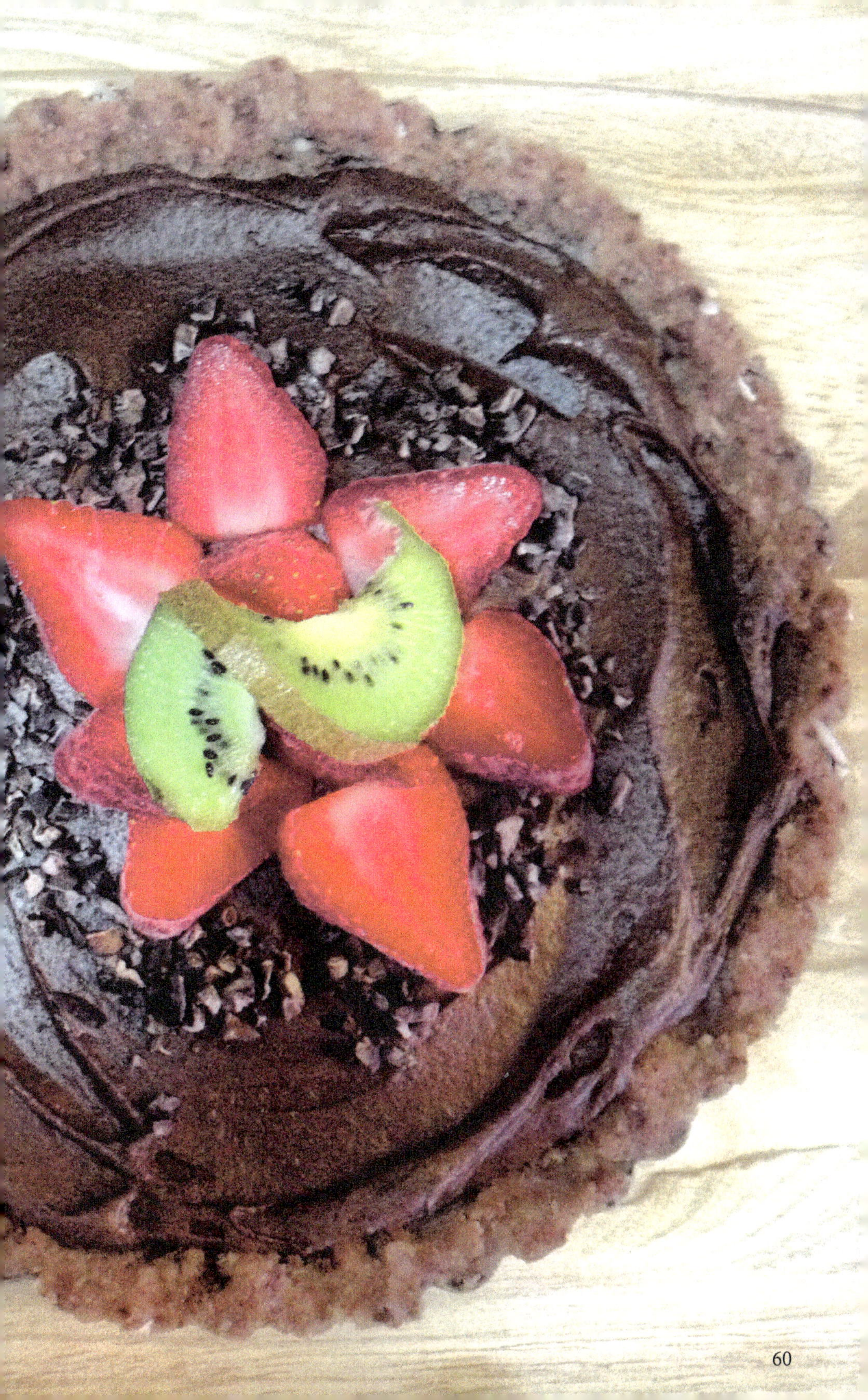

THE FILLING:
- ¾ cup raw cashews, soaked and rinsed
- ½ cup espresso
- 2 tbsp maple syrup
- 1 tbsp lucuma powder
- 1 tbsp mesquite powder
- 1 tsp vanilla powder
- ½ cup raw coconut butter, softened in the dehydrator

THE CRUST:
- ½ cup cashews
- 6 dried figs
- ¼ cup raisins
- ¼ cup of shredded coconut
- 1 tbsp coconut oil, warmed to liquid in the dehydrator
- pinch of vanilla powder
- pinch of pink salt

If you prefer a truly raw cake, sub out espresso for 2 tbsp raw carob powder, and ¼ cup water

salted caramel coffee cake

Procedure for crust:
Pulse nuts first to break them up into smaller bits then add figs until the mix reaches a crumbly consistency. You'll know when it's ready because when you squeeze a little bit in your hand, it will hold together.

Procedure for filling:
Blend in a high-speed blender – don't be afraid to get tough with it. This is the secret to the creamy consistency.

Cake assembly:
Sprinkle a little bit of loose coconut flakes on the bottom of a mini spring-form pan (about four to six inches in diameter) then press the crust mixture into the pan. Pour the filling over the crust and use a spatula to smooth the surface. Garnish with a sprinkle of cacao nibs and a pinch of pink salt. Place the entire cake in the freezer to set (at least three hours). Take out half an hour before serving to thaw.

real fruit roll-ups

INGREDIENTS:
2 BANANAS
2 CUPS RASPBERRIES (FRESH OR FROZEN)
1 TBSP PSYLLIUM HUSK POWDER
1 SQUIRT OF MARINE PHYTOPLANKTON

Procedure:
Blend all ingredients in a high-speed blender. Pour onto Teflex dehydrator sheets, then dehydrate between two to four hours at 145 °F or until the fruit roll is pliable. It should be non-sticky to the touch and a little shiny in appearance. It may need more time if some spots are thicker than others. Once dehydrated yet still pliable (not crispy), they are ready to have the hazelnut cream spread on them. You can then roll them up, slice and serve!

new hazelnut cream

INGREDIENTS:
1 ½ CUPS RAW HAZELNUTS
½ CUP CACAO POWDER
10 MEDJOOL DATES, SOAKED, RINSED AND PITTED
1 CUP WARM WATER
2 TBSP COCONUT OIL, WARMED TO LIQUID IN THE DEHYDRATOR
1 TSP VANILLA EXTRACT
PINCH OF PINK SALT

Procedure:
Add hazelnuts to a food processor and pulse until they acheive a flour-like consistency. Add the remaining ingredients and process until it begins to ball-up like dough.

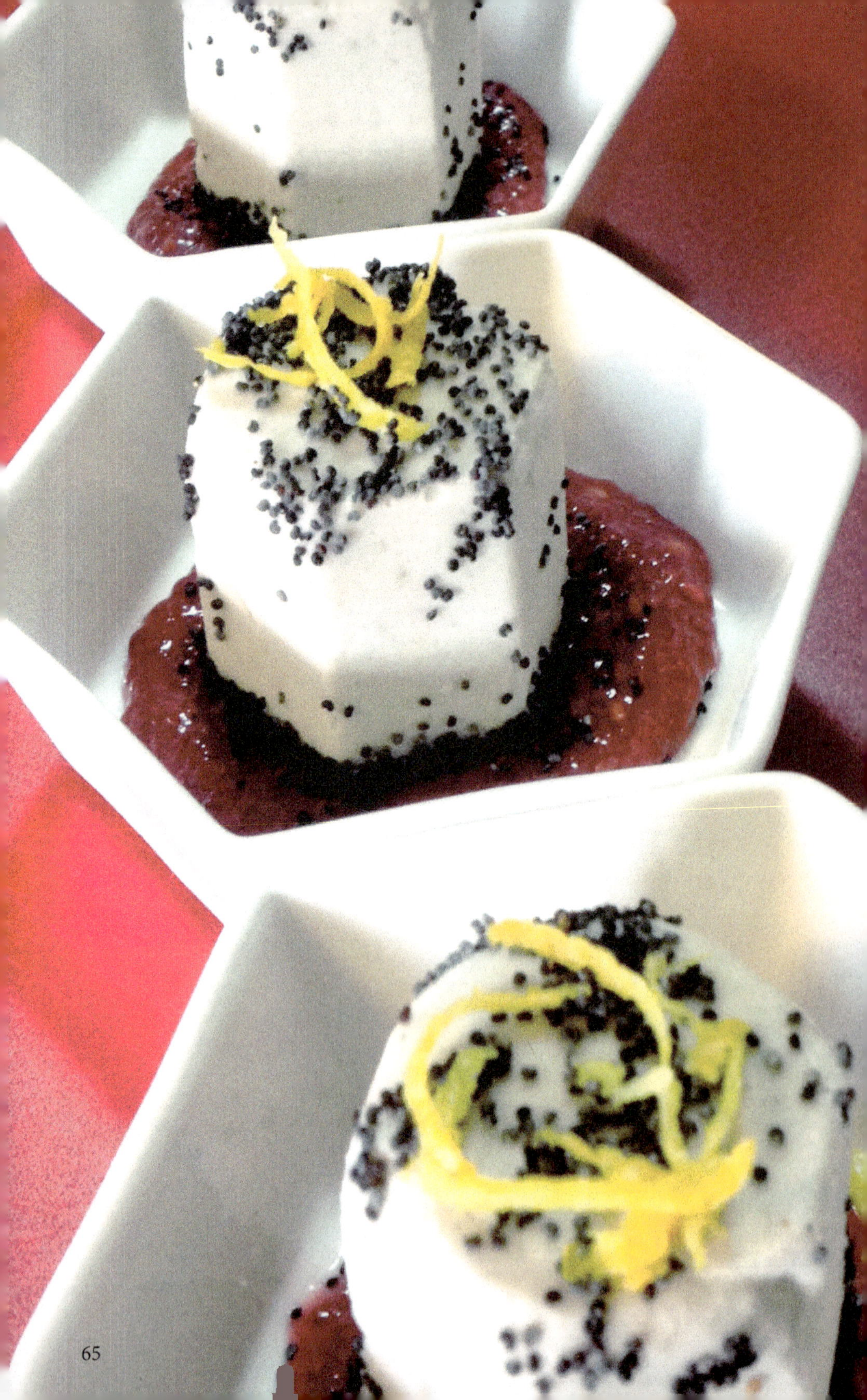

camu camu poppy seed nice cream

INGREDIENTS:
1 CUP YOUNG THAI COCONUT
½ CUP COCONUT BUTTER
1 CUP CASHEWS, SOAKED AND RINSED
½ CUP MAPLE SYRUP
½ CUP LEMON JUICE
1 TBSP LEMON ZEST
2 TSP CAMU CAMU POWDER
1 TBSP POPPY SEEDS, MIX IN BY HAND

GARNISH:
½ CUP RASPBERRIES BLENDED WITH
½ TSBP OF LIQUID SWEETENER AND 1 TBSP CHIA SEEDS
LEMON ZEST

Procedure:
Add all ingredients, except poppy seeds to a high-speed blender. Aerate as necessary. You'll want to make sure the mixture is really creamy. Use a spatula or Vitamix tamper and put some muscle into it! Transfer into a bowl, stir in poppy seeds by hand and pour into ice cream moulds/ice cube trays. Freeze and enjoy! Try it without the cashews for an even creamier nice cream.

What is Camu Camu?

These little berries grow on the camu camu shrub in the lush, swampy riverside of the Amazon. Locals gather them by canoe when the rivers are flooded as the berries weigh heavy on the shrubs and practically fall into the canoes. They are picked in season then sun-dried for medicinal purposes the rest of the year. The purple-reddish berries become light beige when dried and powdered and that's how they are often shipped to us. Due to their enormous amount of vitamin C, they strengthen the immune system, help maintain eyesight and promote healthy skin. Camu camu also supports joint health, decreases inflammation, improves respiratory health, helps with mental clarity and are an anti-stress and anti-anxiety food. Research is being done using the powder to wean people off of antidepressants as well as to calm symptoms of ADHD. This wonder berry can also be used as a natural deodorant and to ward off infections. With a very tangy taste, it blends well with lemon. Use sparingly, as it is quite potent when concentrated into powder form. Blend with juices, smoothies, in salad dressings, ice cream, desserts, or even in your water.

Anti-angiogenics – eat to combat cancer

Cancer is a scary thing. The allopathic treatment of cancer, by cutting, poisoning and burning, leaves a lot to be desired. It is certain that toxins in which we expose ourselves to, willingly or unwillingly, have a hand in developing poor health over the duration of our lives. Even though our bodies are continually fighting these toxins, some will eventually grow into mini-cancer cells. If these cells go unchecked, they may form into tumours. The concept of angiogenesis is how our body is able to generate new blood cells. When blood vessels grow they eventually connect to the tumour and it will begin to grow. This blood supply is a tipping point between a harmless cancer and a harmful one, so one major part of the angiogenesis revolution is to treat cancer by cutting off this blood supply so nothing can grow.

lavender berry surprise pudding

INGREDIENTS:
1 CUP RASPBERRIES
1 CUP BLUEBERRIES
2-3 DATES, PITTED
JUICE OF ½ A LEMON
1/2 CUP CASHEWS, SOAKED AND RINSED
1 TBSP HEMP HEARTS
1 TSP VANILLA POWDER
PINCH OF LAVENDER BUDS
2 CUPS WATER
¾ CUP CHIA SEEDS

Procedure:
Add cashews, dates, berries, lemon, vanilla and lavender to a high-speed blender and blend with water until frothy and creamy. Place chia seeds in a bowl and pour the mixture over top. Stir and let sit for ten to twenty minutes to allow the chia to swell as it takes on a gelatinous state. Serve with a handful of fresh blueberries on top!

Foods such as broccoli, kale, parsley, green tea, garlic, grapes and even lavender have a multitude of cancer-preventative properties. They are considered anti-angiogenic and anti-cancer foods because of their ability to cause apoptosis, the term for when cancer cells self-destruct because of a lack of blood supply.

A few more anti-angiogenic foods include:
- medicinal mushrooms such as reishi, chaga, maitake and shiitake
- the entire allium family including onions and garlic because of high sulphur compounds
- brightly coloured fruits and vegetables loaded with phytonutrients such as citrus fruits and berries
- many herbs and spices including basil, turmeric, cinnamon, nutmeg, licorice, cloves and black pepper
- believe it or not, raw chocolate is also anti-angiogenic!

apple–pear walnut crumble

THE CRUMBLE:
1 CUP WALNUTS
½ CUP OATS
2 TBSP PUMPKIN SEEDS, SOAKED AND RINSED
1 TBSP CHIA SEEDS
2 TSP CINNAMON
1 TSP NUTMEG
PINCH OF CLOVE POWDER
5 DATES, PITTED
PINCH OF PINK SALT

THE FILLING:
3 APPLES
3 PEARS
2 TBSP GROUND FLAX
1 TBSP LIQUID SWEETENER
2 TSP LEMON JUICE
1 TSP CINNAMON

KEEP ONE APPLE FOR THE SECOND-TO-LAST LAYER

Procedure:
In a food processor, mix the crumble ingredients until it acheives a dough-like consistency. Remove from the processor and place in a bowl. Rinse the processor and process the filling ingredients. In a baking dish, press a thick layer of crumble mixture in the bottom of the dish then layer the filling and the remaining crumble mixture one layer at a time. On the second to last layer, place sliced apples, overlapping a little. Top with the last of the crumble. Dehydrate for four hours at 145 °F. Slice or scoop and enjoy with fresh brazil nut mylk (see recipe on page 85)

Honey; nectar of the gods and goddesses, liquid sweetener of choice?

Many believe honey is not "vegan" inspite of the fact that many who would call themselves vegan or "beegan" delight in eating honey for its abundant health benefits and healing properties. This is an on-going debate and both sides have excellent points to make.

From an objective stand point, raw, unfiltered and unpasteurized honey is extremely nutritious and contains a complex array of vitamins and minerals. It is anti-viral, anti-bacterial and anti-fungal. Just be sure to get it from a local, small-scale apiary that cares deeply about their bees. Then you know you are not contributing to a nasty commercial honey business.

If you prefer not to eat honey or other bee products, you have many other choices. Both maple syrup (not raw) and coconut nectar, which is raw, are great alternative sweeteners. Coconut nectar, which is made from the nectar of the coconut palm flower and is extremely sustainable since neither the tree nor the coconuts are harmed when harvested is an excellent choice. Some may choose agave syrup, however there is some controversy surrounding its manufacturing process, so you won't find any recipes within these pages that call for agave. When recipes call for liquid sweetener, you can use honey, coconut nectar or maple syrup, whichever you prefer.

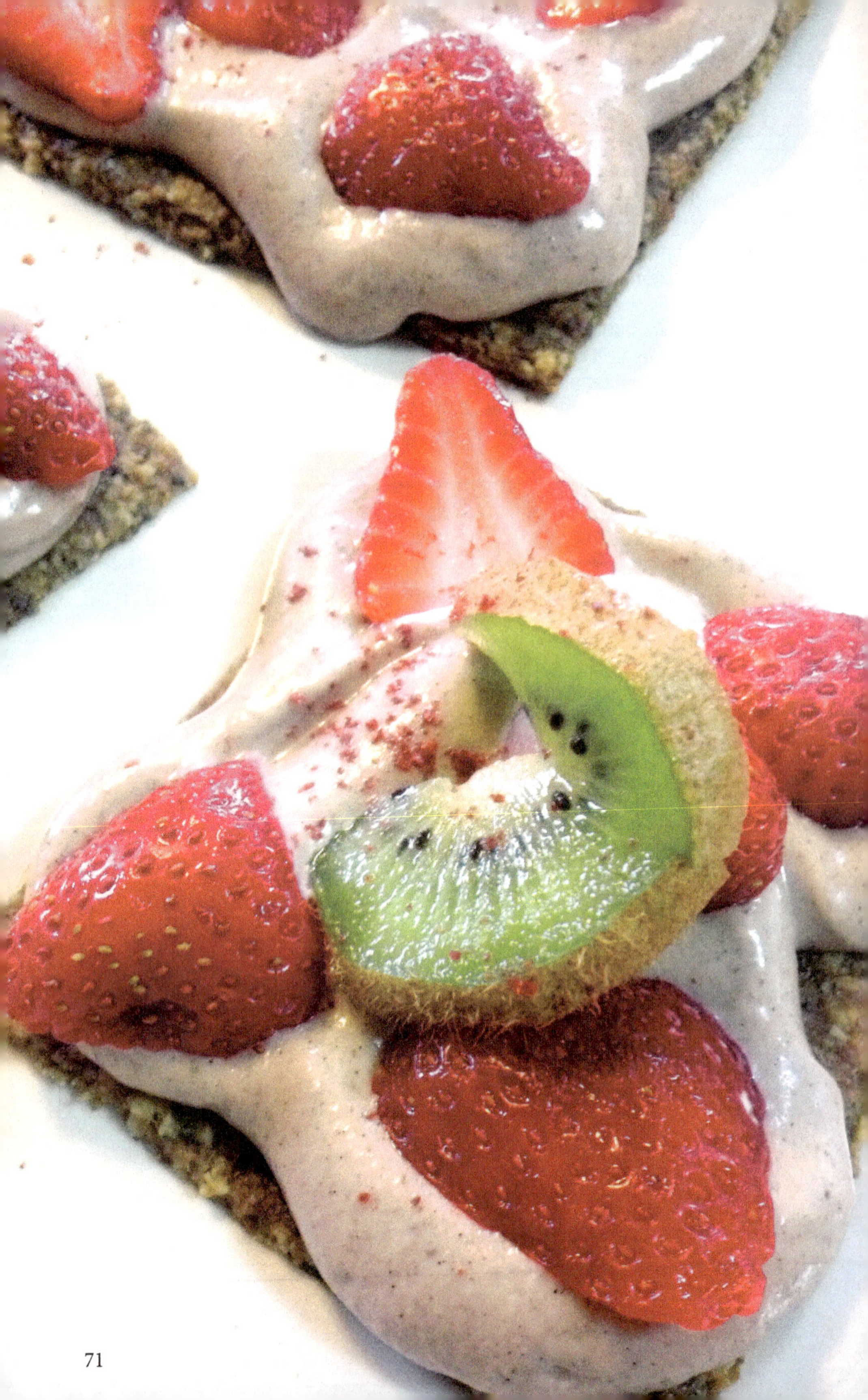

vanilla dream cream

INGREDIENTS:
2 CUPS RAW CASHEWS, SOAKED OVERNIGHT AND DRAINED
1 CUP APPLE, CORED
½ CUP LIQUID SWEETENER
½ CUP WATER, AS NEEDED
3 TSP VANILLA POWDER

Procedure: Blend in a high-speed blender until creamy. Aerate if necessary.

cinnamon apricot bread

INGREDIENTS:
2 CUPS SOAKED APRICOTS (DRIED AND UNSULFURED)
2 CUPS ALMONDS (SPROUTED)
1 CUP PUMPKIN SEEDS (SPROUTED)
1 CUP WATER
½ CUP GROUND FLAX
3 TBSP LIQUID SWEETENER
1 TBSP CINNAMON
1 TSP NUTMEG
PINCH OF PINK SALT

1 CUP RAISINS, SOAKED, MIXED IN BY HAND

Procedure:
Place all ingredients, except the raisins in a food processor and process until well mixed. Transfer dough to a large bowl and mix in raisins by hand. Spread mix onto dehydrator Teflex sheets, just over a quarter-inch thick. Score into square pieces and begin dehydrating at 145°F. After 2 hours, turn the dehydrator down to 110°F, flip the bread and remove Teflex sheets. Continue dehydrating for an additional six to ten hours on mesh screens. The final product should be more pliable than raw crackers due to the dried fruit.

INGREDIENTS:
1 CUP RAW CACAO BUTTER
1 ¼ CUP RAW CACAO POWDER
1 TBSP MACA POWDER
¼ TSP VANILLA POWDER
¼ CUP MAPLE SYRUP OR COCONUT NECTAR*
1 ½ TBSP COCONUT OIL
1 TSP MEDICINAL MUSHROOMS
PINCH OF PINK SALT
5-6 DROPS PEPPERMINT ESSENTIAL OIL (OPTIONAL)

Procedure:
Melt the cacao butter and coconut oil in the dehydrator. Once melted completely, add to the food processor along with the above ingredients and process until a well-mixed paste forms. Work quickly so the mix doesn't solidify on you. Pour the paste into chocolate moulds and refrigerate until hard. Pop them out and enjoy at room temperature with a big smile. You can also make this recipe unflavoured, without the peppermint oil or try with other essential oils such as orange or cinnamon!
*Honey doesn't mix well but when the chocolate solidifies, the cacao butter creates interesting swirls that are quite lovely.

Who Doesn't love Chocolate?

First people who made chocolate were the Mayas and the Aztecs. They drank chocolate as a bitter and spicy beverage called "xocoatl" ("bitter water"). It played an important role in their social and religious life, symbolized life and fertility and was also used as medicine and as a currency. Chocolate in its unprocessed, unheated, raw state is one of the most beneficial health foods we can consume. Commercial chocolate is roasted at such high temperatures that unfortunately they lose important nutrients and volatile oils have the potential to become rancid. Although not fully "raw", since all cacao beans are sun dried and fermented, our choice of cacao is still processed with less energy than its commercial counterparts. It is also usually produced by smaller companies with sustainable sourcing policies, which means that most of it comes from small fair-trade farmers and collectives. Not to be confused with the typical chocolate-flavoured, dairy-packed and sugar-filled "candy" bar, a 6 billion dollar industry today, raw cacao is one of the richest sources of magnesium in a whole food known to us. It also contains phenylethylamine or PEA which has been called "the love molecule". No wonder it has aphrodisiac effects! What is better than making your own raw chocolate from simple ingredients? You can store it for months in the fridge and you'll always have a little snack waiting for you!

before-dinner mint chocolates

"CACAO BEANS ARE PROBABLY THE BEST KEPT
SECRET IN THE ENTIRE HISTORY OF FOOD."
DAVID WOLFE

THE MIGHTY GOJI BERRY

The goji berry has been known for thousands of years in ancient China and Tibet, for both medicinal and culinary uses. These Eastern cultures have revered the tiny berry for its ability to increase strength and longevity as well as support the kidneys and liver through the detoxification process. Nutritionally dense in so many ways, this little berry is truly super! Because goji's contain a wide spectrum of amino acids, including all the essentials, they can be considered to have one of the highest concentrations of protein found in fruit. Like many of the superfoods found within this book, the goji is a powerful antioxidant, combating free radicals and keeping our cells healthier for longer.

A note of caution... most organic goji berries on the market come from China, where "organic" laws are not as strict as they should be. Buy yours from a reputable source.

goji berry orange fudge

INGREDIENTS:
¾ CUP GOJI BERRIES
¼ CUP RAW ALMOND BUTTER
½ CUP RAW CACAO POWDER
½ CUP LIQUID SWEETENER
1 TBSP VIRGIN COCONUT OIL
1 TBSP ORANGE ZEST OR
2 DROPS WILD ORANGE ESSENTIAL OIL (OPTIONAL)
2 TSP VANILLA POWDER
PINCH OF PINK SALT

Procedure:
In a food processor, bust up the goji berries until they are roughly chopped. Then add the rest of the ingredients and process until smooth. If you chill this mixture before working with it, it is easier to handle. Depending on the consistency of the fudge, you may either scoop the mixture with a small ice cream scoop and hand roll into balls or spoon it onto parchment paper and refrigerate until solid. These make an awesome gift, so share with all those you love - that's if you can save some!

ESSENTIAL OILS IN THE RAW PLANT-BASED DIET

Essential oils are powerful aromatic compounds extruded from the seeds, bark, stems, roots, flowers, and other parts of plants. They can be used aromatically in diffusers, topically for massages and internally for use in delicious recipes, like many found in this book. Not only do they add a unique spark to the culinary genius of raw food preparation, but each oil can have hundreds of different compounds and each compound has a different medicinal benefit. Pharmaceutical companies actually mimic natural compounds found in certain plants yet over 250,000 North Americans die each year from pharmaceuticals. Why mess with nature? Nature has it right from the start. Look for 100% therapeutic-grade oils that test to ensure they are beyond organic, pure, genuine, authentic and potent, free from fillers and foreign contaminants.

no-bake coconut cashew rawkies

INGREDIENTS:
2 CUPS ROLLED OATS
1 CUP CASHEWS
1 CUP DATES
½ CUP COCONUT BUTTER
½ CUP COCONUT FLAKES
3 TBSP COCONUT OIL, WARMED TO LIQUID IN THE DEHYDRATOR
1 TBSP MACA POWDER
1 TBSP MESQUITE POWDER
½ TSP VANILLA
¼ TSP PINK SALT
1 CUP RAW CHOCOLATE CHUNKS, MIXED IN BY HAND

*MAKE THE RAW CHOCOLATE RECIPE FOUND ON PAGE 73, BUT LEAVE OUT THE PEPPERMINT ESSENTIAL OIL

Procedure:
Melt the coconut butter and coconut oil in the dehydrator at 118°F and set aside. Bust up the rest of the dry ingredients in the food processor then slowly add the liquid coconut while spinning. It should all mix well. Break or cut up the raw chocolate and mix in by hand. Roll into balls and chill for a few hours. These will keep in your freezer for many weeks - if you can restrain yourself!

COCONUT POWER!

Coconut is one of the world's most abundant and sustainable crops, growing in at least ninety tropical countries around the world. The coconut palm has been respected and utilized by many different cultures in many ways - from the creation of textiles from coconut fibre to the building of fences by weaving the leaves together to the creation of bowls and jewelry from the hard shell. From a health perspective, the coconut definitely is a superfood with many benefits beyond its nutritional content. Whether it's the water, oil or inner flesh, in its raw state, the whole coconut is rich in enzymes designed to help detoxify and repair the body. Being compatible with human blood, coconut water can be administered intravenously to prevent the detrimental effects or even death caused by severe dehydration. It was used this way in the Vietnam war where it saved hundreds of lives. Because coconut water is the ultimate thirst quencher, it boosts hydration via electrolytes. There is also growing evidence that the daily consumption of coconut oil can combat the onset of Alzheimer's and support the thyroid. Some cultures even believe the oil to be the cure for all illness. With a wide and complex array of nutrients, coconut can have profoundly positive effects on health when it is eaten on a regular basis. I like to use the oil on my face as a moisturizer, mixed with one drop each of lavender, peppermint and tea tree oil as well as adding a dollop to my tea in the morning.

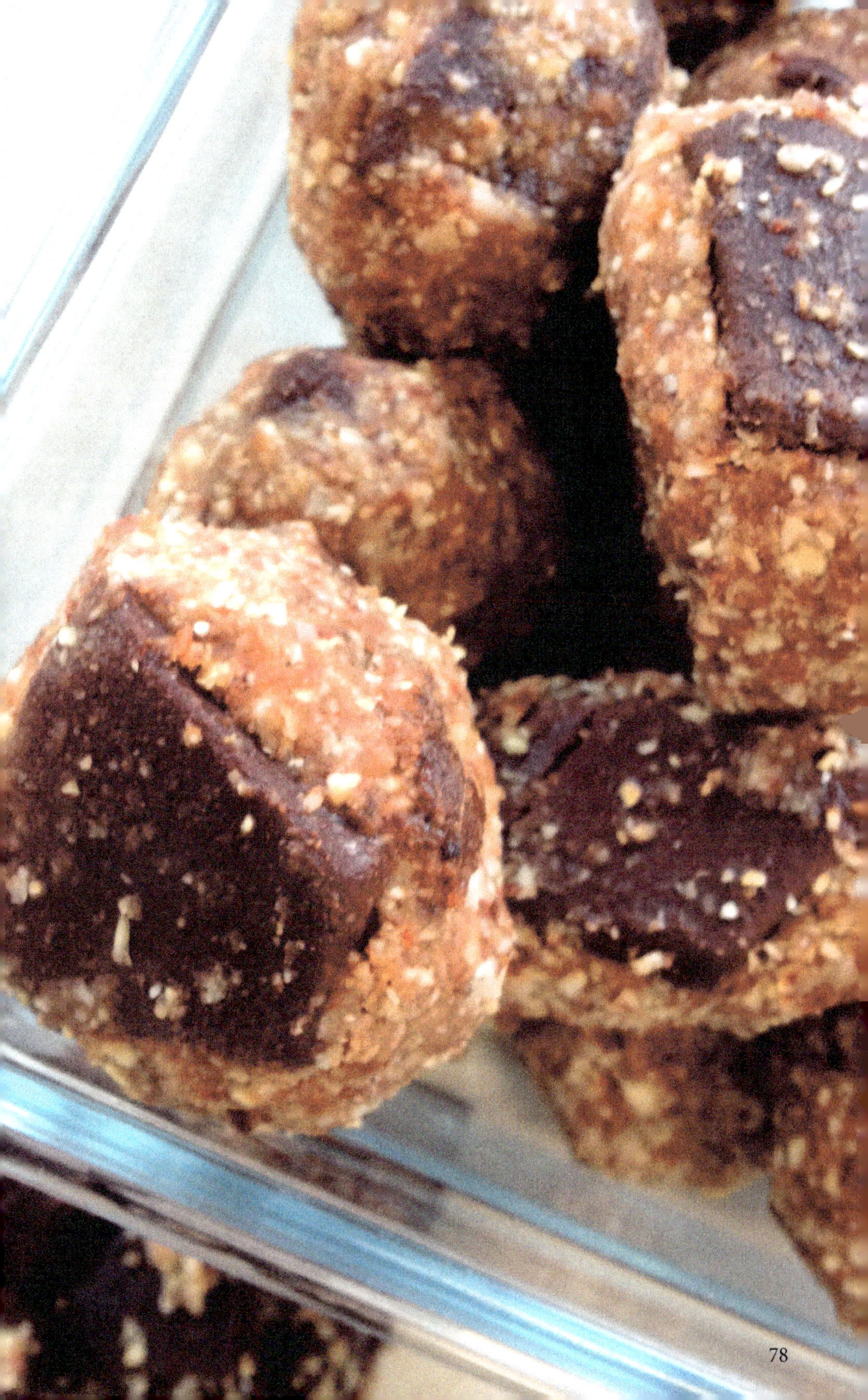

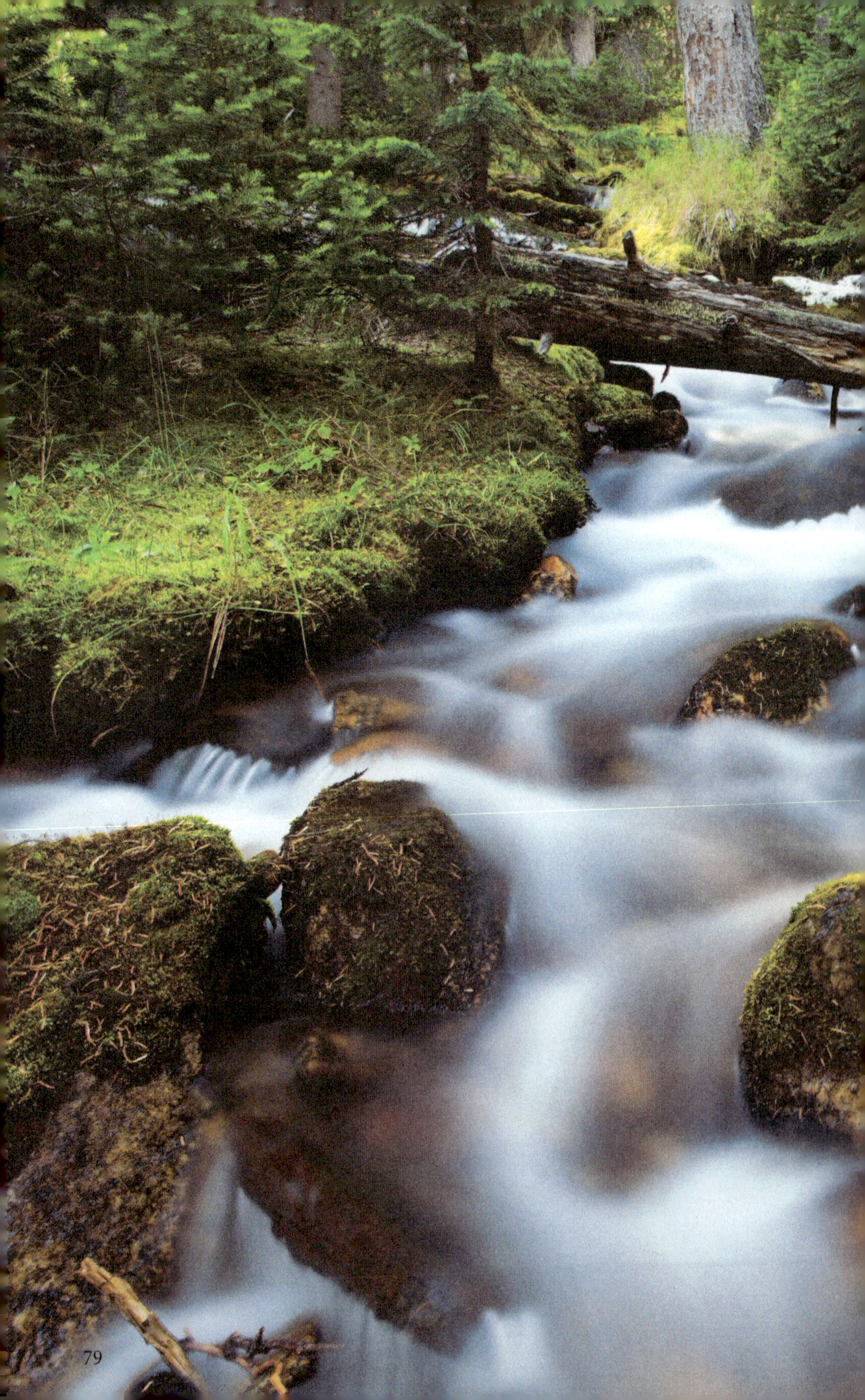

To Quench Thirst

rooibos kombucha bubble tea

THE SCOBY ←

This tangy, effervescent health drink is made from fermented sweetened tea. Kombucha acts as an immediate digestive tonic, much like apple cider vinegar. It colonizes the gut with friendly bacteria and yeasts, detoxifies the liver and cleans and rejuvenates the digestive system as a whole. It's health benefits are outrageous! You can get a SCOBY (Symbiotic Colony of Bacteria and Yeast) from a friend or check online for a dehydrated culture - try upayanaturals.com, a Canadian-based raw, vegan superstore. The SCOBY acts as the starter culture for the fermentation process and is an essential ingredient in making an awesome kombucha brew.

INGREDIENTS:
ONE KOMBUCHA SCOBY AND ½ CUP STARTER TEA FROM A PREVIOUS BATCH OF KOMBUCHA, OR 2 CUPS FROM A STORE-BOUGHT BATCH - NON-FLAVOURED
4 TEA BAGS (ROOIBOS, BLACK, GREEN OR WHITE TEA – DO NOT USE TEAS WITH FLAVOURING AS THIS WILL INTERFERE WITH THE FERMENTATION PROCESS
¼ CUP COCONUT SUGAR OR RAW CANE SUGAR – BUT NOT HONEY AS IT WON'T FERMENT DUE TO ITS ANTI-BACTERIAL PROPERTIES
4 CUPS FILTERED WATER

EQUIPMENT:
1-LITRE MASON JAR
PLASTIC OR WOOD STIRRING UTENSIL
BREATHABLE COVER FOR THE JAR
SUCH AS A TIGHT-WEAVE DISH TOWEL
RUBBER BAND TO SECURE THE TOWEL

Once the kombucha is made and ready to "flavour", add the following and stir:

1 ½ CUP FERMENTED KOMBUCHA TEA
½ CUP STRONG BREWED ROOIBOS TEA
2 TBSP WHOLE CHIA SEEDS

Within minutes, the chia seeds will swell and settle at the bottom of the cup. Stir a few times as they are swelling and enjoy chilled!

Procedure: Place hot water and sugar together in a jar. Mix until the sugar dissolves. Place the tea in this mix and steep for ten minutes, remove, then cool to room temperature. Once cooled, place the kombucha SCOBY and 'starter tea' (extra kombucha liquid) into the sweet tea (if the tea is too hot, it will kill the SCOBY). Cover the jar with the towel and rubber band so it can still breathe but is sealed. When making kombucha, it is important to wash and rinse your hands and all equipment well prior to working with the tea mixture or the SCOBY. Be thoroughly clean and give everything an extra rinse.

Fermenting the kombucha: Choose a warm place between 70° and 80°F out of sunlight with a reasonably good airflow. Keep away from any other cultured foods as cross-contamination by stray yeasts and bacteria can be problematic. It is important to allow the kombucha to ferment undisturbed. Moving the jar will not ruin the batch, but it will take longer to ferment.

Waiting: Your brew may be ready in five to seven days. For the first few batches, start tasting on day seven, but again, remember that cleanliness is of utmost important. Go with your own personal taste preferences. Some people like it best after only a week, whereas I prefer about four weeks of fermentation. Shorter fermentation will result in a sweeter brew. Longer periods will result in a more vinegar-like taste. The longer the brew ferments, the less sugar will remain, so if sugar consumption is a concern, ferment longer.

How do I know if my kombucha is ready?: You will begin to notice the formation of a new "baby" SCOBY. This process begins as a thin layer of film developing on the surface of the liquid. Over time it will grow thicker until it resembles a floating cake. As the kombucha ferments, the SCOBY will consume the sugar and produce acids, vitamins, enzymes, and carbon dioxide. As this process proceeds, the brew will taste less sweet and more acidic.

Normal variations: Each batch of kombucha is unique. Naturally, the SCOBY may float, sink to the bottom or hover in the middle of the brew. You may see a brown stringy substance floating in the container, sediment forming at the bottom or brown blobs clinging to the SCOBY. All of this is normal.

Signs of potential problems: The acidic nature of the brew makes it very uncommon for mold to develop. However, the most common cause of mold is forgetting an ingredient or not being clean enough. If you see white, green, orange, red, or black round spots on top of the SCOBY, you may have mold. In this case, you should compost it and begin again. If your kombucha doesn't seem to be fermenting, it may be in a place that is too cool. While it is quite rare for a batch to fail, if it happens, just throw it out and start over.

Harvesting your kombucha: Now you're ready to enjoy your brew. Remove the SCOBY, making sure to be very clean. You'll need to make a new batch of sugar tea with some starter kombucha so you will have a place to put both the original SCOBY you started with as well as the baby SCOBY that formed during the fermentation process. If you want to share the love, you can tear the SCOBY apart and divide it in order to start new cultures in separate containers.

Bottling for later: If you'd like, kombucha can be bottled for consumption at a later date. The active yeast and bacteria in the kombucha continue to process the remaining tea and sugar in the brew even in the absence of the SCOBY. This process means that a new baby SCOBY may start to form again over time. The fermentation process produces carbon dioxide, which will build up under pressure and give it some fizziness. Be careful of explosions! If you keep the kombucha refrigerated, you should avoid any accidents.

lemon molasses kefir

Time frame: thirty-six to fourty-eight hours
Special Equipment:
Clean Glass 2-litre jar
Cloth to cover and an elastic band
Non-metal strainer or nut milk bag

Ingredients:
4 cups water - tap water left to sit (to off-gas the chlorine) or if you have access to alkaline water, even better
2 tbsp molasses
2 tbsp coconut sugar or raw cane sugar, honey won't work as it's antibacterial
2 teaspoons water kefir grains*
2 slices organic lemon

*Just like kombucha, kefir needs a starter culture to create its fermened magic. Ask around or look online for kefir "grains" as the starter culture.

Procedure:
If using a large grain sugar, dissolve it in a little warm water and let it cool first before adding it to the rest of the water and kefir grains. Pour this and the rest of the water and the molasses into a sterilized glass jar and drop the kefir grains in. Add the lemon slices at the end and swirl.

Do not tighten a lid over the jar. Keep the air flowing. Wrap a towel over and around the jar and keep in a warm place for thirty-six to fourty-eight hours. During this time, you can periodically agitate the grains. The kefir should turn cloudy, having become probiotic-rich. It should taste a little bit sweet with an after taste of flat beer or cider. You may have to repeat the process all over again if all you taste is sweet water after thirty-six to fourty-eight hours. Usually, the grains take time to adjust in their new home. Strain the water kefir into a separate glass jar and store in the fridge or use it immediately in a smoothie.

Rinse the kefir grains and store them in a small glass jar in the fridge with a concentrated sugar water, or use them immediately in another batch. You may also dehydrate them at room temperature for long-term storage.

For more detail on making your own kefir: www.yemoos.com/waterkefirguide.html

Kefir, a story of intrigue

"Kefir grains were treasured by the people who possessed them, passed down from generation to generation, and definitely not shared with strangers.

Early in the twentieth century, the "All Russian Physicians' Society" became interested in obtaining the mysterious source of this healthful drink. Since the keepers of the grains did not wish to share them, this required deception and culture thievery. The scheme involved a young Russian woman named Irina Sakharova, whom the physicians hoped would be able to charm a Caucasus prince, Bek-Mirza Barchorov, into giving her some kefir grains. He refused, she tried to leave, he had her kidnapped, she was rescued, and he was charged in the Czar's courts. For reparations, the young woman was awarded the treasure she sought; the court ordered the prince to give her some of his cherished kefir grains. In 1908, she brought the first kefir grains to Moscow. Kefir became, and remains to this day, a popular drink in Russia. In 1973, at age 85, Irina Sakharova was formally recognized by the Soviet Ministry of Health for her role in bringing kefir to the Russian people."
~ an excerpt from *Wild Fermentation* by Sandor Ellix Katz.

SHILAJIT, ROCK WARRIOR

Very fitting for me, as a rock climber I was drawn to Shilajit, which means rock warrior in Sanskrit, the Indian equivalent of Latin. This Ayurvedic superfood is a smoky-flavoured mineral pitch that oozes of ancient rock formations particularly in the Himalayas and Hindu Kush regions of India. As an adaptogen, shilajit helps bring our bodies toward homeostasis and allows us to resist extreme environments where cold and higher altitudes are of concern. Loaded with medicinal humic and fulvic acids, it supports deep rejuvenation and enhances our energy production on a cellular level. Add it to anything chocolate and feel the buzz of peak performance and enhanced stamina.

fresh brazil nut mylk

INGREDIENTS:
2 CUPS RAW BRAZIL NUTS, SOAKED FOR 24 HOURS AND RINSED TWICE
4 CUPS WATER, DIVIDED
A PINCH OF CARDAMOM
½ TBSP LIQUID SWEETENER

Procedure:
Drain the Brazil nuts, rinse well and put them in the blender with ine and a half cups of fresh water, blending with less water in the beginning makes for a smoother paste. When smooth, add the remaining water and blend until frothy. Strain through a cheesecloth or nut milk bag, squeezing to release all the milk into a large bowl. Transfer to a glass jar and keep in the fridge for up to four days.

chocolate warrior latte

Ingredients:
½ cup coconut butter
¼ cup raw cacao powder
¼ cup raw honey
2 tbsp cacao nibs
2 tbsp coconut oil
2 drops of cinnamon esential oil
½ tsp chipotle powder
1 squirt of marine phytoplankton
6 cups hot water

Add another superfood (or two) to your latte;
½ tbsp maca
1 tsp shilajit
1 tsp medicinal mushroom powder

Procedure:
Combine all of the above in a high-speed blender and blend on high until frothy and warm.

ACID AND ALKALINE; A DELICATE BALANCE

Your body's acid/alkaline chemistry is responsible for weight loss, increased stamina and strength, and a stronger immune system. A body that is acidic is more prone to develop auto immune diseases such as diabetes, arthritis, heart disease and cancer. The body is affected on a cellular level. Acidity also enhances inflammation, raises cortisol levels and impairs sleep. All life-giving chemical reactions happen when electrons are paired. Whereas all damaging reactions happen when they are not paired, such as is the case with free radicals. Whole foods are electron balancing and eliminate free radicals by way of antioxidants. They are also highly alkaline by nature. When you give the body what it needs, it can properly maintain this delicate acid/alkaline balance. Maintaining a balance of 75% alkaline foods and 25% acidic foods is ideal. Some fruits, such as citrus, have an acidic pH outside of the body, but when consumed, leave an alkaline residue in the body after being metabolized. To protect our blood and keep it in balance, the body steals alkaline minerals such as calcium and magnesium from our bones, thus making them weaker. Your body fights hard to neutralize acids and maintain the proper pH in organs, tissues and body fluids. An easy way to accomplish this is to make fruits and vegetables the main part of each meal.

green beauty smoothie

Ingredients:
2 ripe bananas
1 cup pineapple, chopped
4 handfuls baby spinach
1 medjool date, pitted
2 tsp lemon zest
2 tsp maca powder
1 tsp spirulina powder
3 cups water

Procedure for the smoothie:
Blend in a high-speed blender until frothy

blood builders brew

Ingredients:
1 red beetroot
1 carrot
1 tomato
1 cucumber
2 cups pineapple, chopped
1 whole lemon

lust for life elixir

Ingredients:
4 stalks celery
1 cucumber
2 big handfuls kale
A thumb sized piece of ginger
1 whole lemon
3 apples (fuji or gala)
½ serrano, seeds removed

Procedure for the brew and elixir:
Process through a juicer and serve within half an hour for optimal freshness!

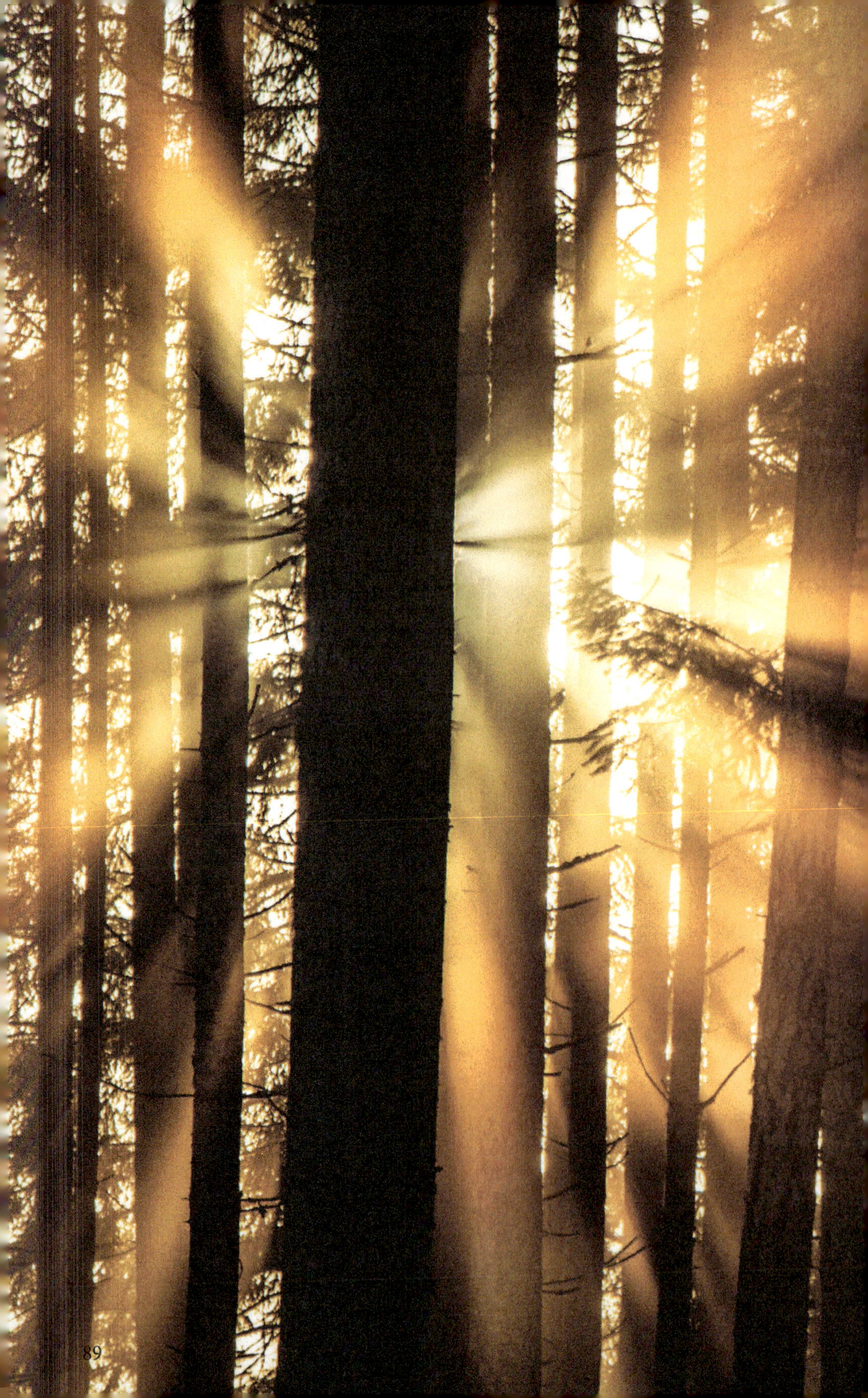

no matter how many trees,
you can still see the sun
shining through

WHERE DO YOU GET YOUR PROTEIN?

We've been told our whole lives that we eat to gain protein for strong muscles and calcium for strong teeth. The fact is, we don't eat to gain protein, carbohydrates or fats, we eat to gain energy. Unfortunately, many of us have become disconnected from our food and know little of what takes place between farm and plate. We think of nutrition in terms of the elements that we need, calcium from milk, vitamin A from carrots, etc. Where these nutrients come from has been influenced by those with money and power. Why is it that the FDA is funded by agribusiness and yet they are also the ones who regulate "recommended daily allowances" and the entire structure of the food pyramid? I would call this a conflict of interest. Big agribusiness wants us to associate protein with beef and calcium with milk. The most common argument in favour of eating meat is that it is necessary to build and maintain strength, yet the strongest animals in the world (elephants, oxen, gorillas) eat only grasses and fruit. The human body builds protein from the eight essential amino acids and the original source of these amino acids is not animal flesh, it's from vegetation that the animals get theirs. Why not skip the middle man and go straight to the source?

Brendan Brazier, former professional Ironman triathlete, bestselling author and formulator of award-winning plant-based Vega nutritional products has researched plant-based protein to the nth-degree. "Because both your health and environment matter, the nutrient-to-resource ratio considers the micronutrient gain from the food and natural resources required to produce the food. By far, plant-based foods require the least amount of resources to produce and deliver the most nutrients." If you look at this research from a purely scientific point of view, it can't be refuted. In regards to both health and the environment, plant-based protein sources are the way to go. Brazier's research in his book **The Thrive Diet** concludes that "choosing a plant-based diet is the single biggest possible environmental impact you can make as an individual. Aside from the significant health benefits, a plant-based diet can reduce your carbon footprint (CO_2 emissions) more than changing your daily commute."

But, organic, free range meats that are raised in a sustainable way are much better than factory farmed fodder, right? This is true in so many ways, but even organically raised and "happy" animals are hard to digest and are higher in toxins than any plant food. Let's compare ourselves with a well known carnivore, the lion. Lions have sharp teeth, powerful stomach acid and short digestive tracts in order to chew, digest and assimilate all the animal protein that they need to survive. They also spend a lot of time lazing around digesting. No way would our square molars be able to chew so much animal protein in a day. Our jaws and teeth are more suited for grinding plant matter. Our stomach acid is not strong enough to fully break down animal proteins to their smallest particles in order for us to digest and assimilate. When proteins go undigested, there is a chance we may suffer an auto-immune response or allergic reaction as the body may see these undigested proteins as foreign objects to attack. This goes for plant proteins too, so chew your food. Sometimes these allergic reactions are delayed. Next time you are feeling ill, think about what you ate in the last forty-eight hours.

Unfortunately, we are so consumed with this idea of protein that most of us are getting too much. What's wrong with that?

Animal proteins in large amounts cause our pH to become more acidic. Disease thrives in an acidic environment. Since our bodies are slightly alkaline to begin with, we must strive to keep this balance. Our body, miracle that it is, is left with no choice but to draw out the alkaline minerals such as calcium and magnesium from our bones in order to buffer the acid. There are studies that show countries whose inhabitants consume diets high in animal protein and dairy in fact have a higher incidence of osteoporosis, a degeneration of the bones caused by calcium deficiency. This scientific fact shows that even though we are drinking so much milk, we, in fact, have weaker bones.

Our nutrition is controlled by the efficiency of our digestive system and by what our bodies do with that food or how bioavailable this food is to us. Bioavailability is the rate at which your body can absorb nutrients and use them to benefit your health. Whole, plant-based foods are easy to digest and much more bioavailable than animal-based proteins. Without enzymes and a healthy digestive system, food cannot be turned into usable nutrients for the body. When a plant has a full spectrum of amino acids, it creates a complete protein. Colin T. Campbell, a doctor on the forefront of plant-based nutrition believes, "plant proteins are somewhat compromised by their limitation of one or more amino acids. When we restore the relatively deficient amino acid in a plant protein, we get a response rate equivalent to animal proteins." So, by eating a variety of unrefined grains, legumes, seeds, nuts, and vegetables throughout the day, the deficit of one food low in a particular essential amino acid will be made up by another food.

I love spending time in the beautiful, great, wondrous outdoors. With barefeet touching the earth, I welcome the wind, rain, sun and all of what nature has to offer.

As you visit the most pristine natural places that this great globe has to offer, tread lightly :)

all-natural bug spray

INGREDIENTS:
2 CUPS WITCH HAZEL
2 TBSP NEEM OIL – WHICH CONTAINS NATURAL INSECTICIDAL COMPOUNDS

50 DROPS ESSENTIAL BLEND:
10 DROPS CITRONELLA
10 DROPS CEDARWOOD
10 DROPS LEMONGRASS
10 DROPS LAVENDER
5 DROPS LEMON
5 DROPS EUCALYPTUS

Procedure: Add all ingredients to a spray bottle, shake, spray, repeat!

This stuff really works!

I make my own insect repellent and it has worked wonders for me while bush-whacking through dense forest, climbing vertical peaks, canoeing grand lakes, slogging through the desert and even in my own back yard at the height of pesky bug season. It may not work as well as pure Deet, but you'll feel much better about drenching yourself with the stuff rather than its chemical counterpart. And it sure smells lovely!

a special thank you

My lovely family whom I love with all my heart, my mom Theresa, my father Bob, my sisters Lauren and Marinna and my brother Alex - you are always there and have always been there for me no matter what crazy ideas I come up with

My inspirations:
Wayne Parker, an exemplary human being, David "Avocado" Wolfe, the late Holly Mauro, Brendan Brazier and all the plant-based athletes out there, Christian Griffith, Taylor Conroy and the Journey Team, for their passion to make the world a better place, Daphne MacDonald, an amazing mother and friend, Lydia Zamorano, for your dedication to sharing the most beautiful things in life, Stefano Tricanico, for following your heart, Vanja Kurucz, Clara Hughes, an inspiration to all Canadians, rock climbing sensations, Sean Villanueva O'Driscoll, Nico Favresse and Sonnie Trotter, Theresa Mowat, Daniel Gurule, Sam Katzman, Lauren Bedard, Danielle Love, Bethiah Rosa, Nessa Goldman, Lila Smith, Georgette Paré, Dr. Wayne Dyer, Lao Tzu, Buddha

To all the beautiful women and men that have taken my certification courses, for your continued support and encouraging kindness.

My kitchen comrade and co-author of the Kitchens of Pinch and Dash series, Jessica Perlaza

Nea Ramos, the most amazing virtual assistant one could ever dream of

Alicia Severson and her amazing cover art
http://aliciaseverson.blogspot.ca/

The talented chef, Corinna Haight, for editing the rough draft and all the extra advice

The late Ann Wigmore and all the staff at The Ann Wigmore Institute

All those who contributed to the online Indiegogo campaign

The photographers, Stefano Tricanico, Jonathan Huyer, Alan Denis, Seon Hwa Shim, Johanna Guinard, Jessica Perlaza, Jill LaBelle Sophie Shouldice and Gillian Shepherd who have shared their amazing photos

www.seashepherd.org for inspiring me to believe in something worthwhile - saving our oceans

Those who bought sauerkraut out of my van and trusted that it would be the most delicious thing they ever ate!

Recipes inspired by and adapted from the Raw Foundation Culinary Arts Institute
www.rawfoundation.ca
Pad Thai Salad ~ page 19
Lentil Dippers ~ page 35
Real Fruit Roll-ups ~ page 63
Hazelnut Cream ~ page 64

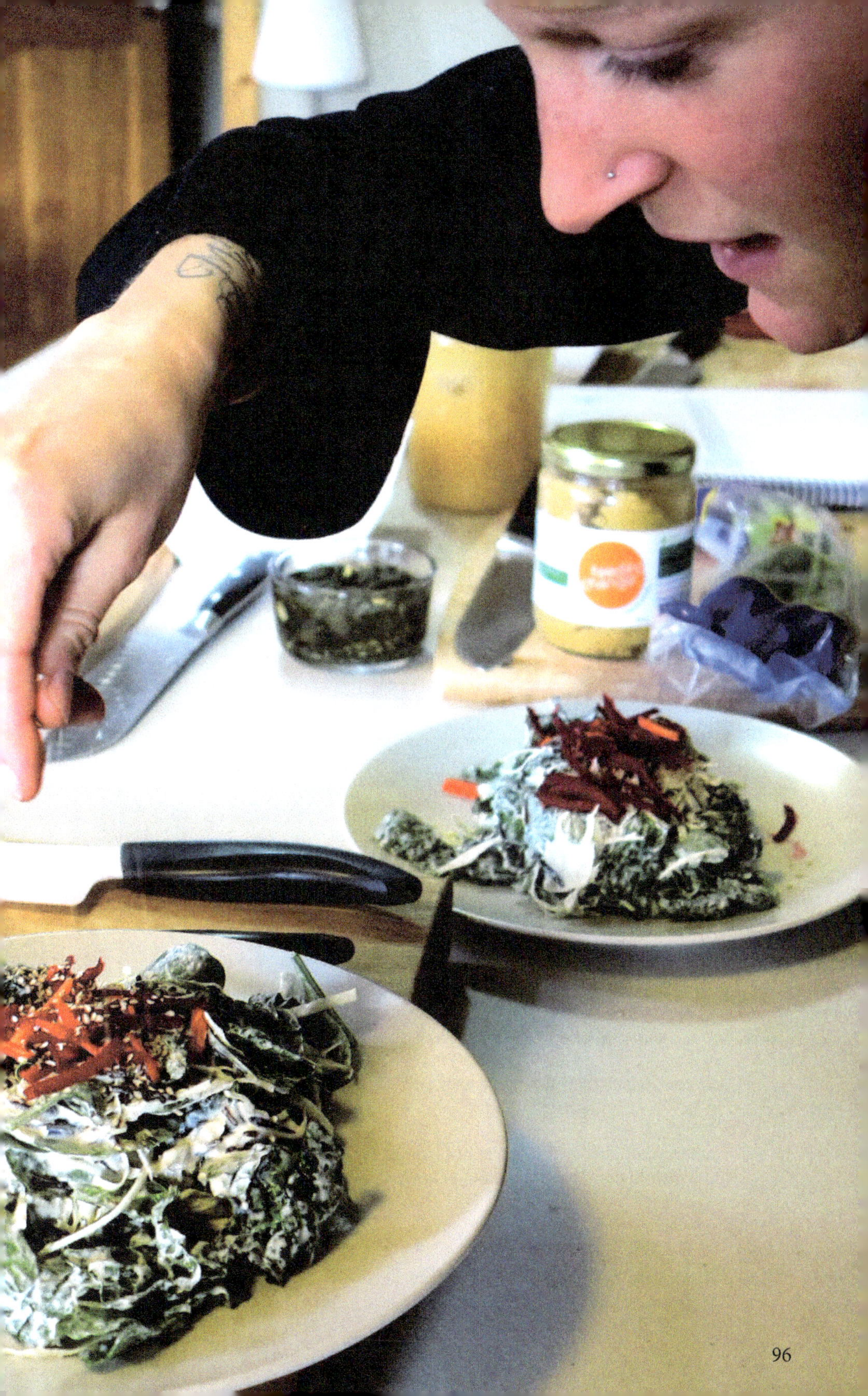

Once neighbours who went knocking on each other's doors to borrow a pinch of this and a dash of that, these two ladies were full of passion who discovered a mutual love for cooking and sharing. And so Danielle Arsenault and Jessica Perlaza became the Kitchens of Pinch and Dash, creating a seasonal cookbook series, full of heart-warming food, photos, poetry and anecdotes inspired by the seasons that so greatly influence the way they eat and live. All recipes are vegan and gluten free and were created, tasted and photographed by both ladies.

May your table always be filled with good food and great friends!

www.thekitchensofpinchanddash.blogspot.ca
https://issuu.com/thekitchensofpinchanddash